2007 PRESIDENTIAL ADDRESS

TICKET COLLECTING ALONG A 'CUL de SAC'

given by

KEN PUDSEY

To a meeting of the Society at
Southwick Community Centre,
Southwick, West Sussex
on 23rd February 2008

and subsequently repeated in two parts at
The Friends Meeting House,
Mount Street,
Manchester.

1st March 2008 (North Bank and River Traffic)
and 13th December 2008 (South Bank)

An extract of this presentation was also given
in Rotterdam on 18th October 2008

The Transport Ticket Society
2012

*The production of this publication has also been made possible thanks
to the bequest to the Society by the late Courtney Haydon
who was a member for about 34 years*

*Further copies of this and other Publications may be obtained from the
Society's Publication Sales Officer:*

Steve Skeavington
6 Breckbank,
Forest Town,
MANSFIELD.
NG19 0PZ

*Comments etc. regarding this publication are welcome;
please write to the Hon. Secretary,*

Alan Peachey
4 The Sycamores,
BISHOPS STORTFORD.
CM23 5JR

Published by

The Transport Ticket Society
4 The Sycamores,
Bishops Stortford.
CM23 5JR.

© Ken Pudsey 2012

ISBN 978-0-903209-72-4

Printed by

Pureprint Group
Bellbrook Park
UCKFIELD
TN22 1PL

We gratefully acknowledge permission given by Ordnance Survey, Southampton
for allowing the reproduction of the map on the front page of this publication.

Ticket Collecting Along a 'Cul de Sac'

Introduction

Good afternoon Gentlemen. May I first thank everyone for bestowing the Honour of President on me for the current year.

I have been collecting tickets seriously for 45 years and been a member of The Transport Ticket Society for 42 years. Some of you may be aware that my father was a very early member of the Ticket and Fare Collection Society, joining in 1947, but discontinuing membership when studying for a career after army days, took up all his time. It was he, in fact whose name was on the membership list when I joined in 1966, as I was too young for the rules in those days.

My current other roles in The Transport Ticket Society are Index Editor for UK and Irish Road Operators since 1980 and UK Road Ticket Acquisitions Officer since 2002.

Enough of the self, what about the title of the talk.

'Ticket Collecting Along A 'Cul de Sac'?'
What does this mean?

For all but nine months of my life, I have lived by the Humber Estuary. If you look at the road and rail networks along the Humber, Hull where I was born, is at the end of a 30 mile long 'Cul de Sac' (M62/A63) and Cleethorpes, where I now live, is at the end of an even longer one, at 44 miles (M180/A180). In both cases this is how far you have to travel before joining the country's main transport infrastructure. Heading directly North from Hull or South from Cleethorpes can only be regarded as "local". In fact as far as the Railway Companies are concerned this is emphasised even more. Most Scarborough and all Bridlington Trans-pennine services normally go via Hull and this involves a reversing movement. There are, however, some Scarborough trains that go via Malton and York. Cleethorpes to anywhere except Barton-on-Humber, involves travelling via Doncaster other than the three trains via Lincoln to the Midlands (none on Sundays). Emphasised by the fact that to attend a Committee meeting in Birmingham in November 2007, the route offered was via Doncaster and not Lincoln!

Whilst not an area prolific with bus operators when compared with the hey day of County Durham or Bus Wars in Manchester or Greenock, there have been some gems along the way. This talk is not meant to be a definitive survey of tickets from the area, more a personal recollection of what has been and what is available in this sleepy corner of England. Although the Humber is a large barrier between the two banks of the river which were not physically joined until 1981, it will be shown that this did not keep the transport operators, both road and rail firmly entrenched on one side or the other. The tangled web of some of the bus operator's post 1986 is probably not fully unmeshed even today.

Bus, Rail, Ferry, Intermodal and other tickets will be featured, together with some interesting tickets used in relation to an Aircraft factory just outside Hull, which is currently very busy, and has started flying its finished aircraft again from Brough, instead of transporting in kit form to Warton. Air Traffic Control facilities are provided by Humberside Airport at Kirmington.

If your specialist interest in the Road field is Stock Tickets, then this is the place to be: from punch, untitled TIM, Almex A to Wayfarer, and TRANSPORT SERVICES Ultimate there are plenty of stock/untitled tickets to be had around these parts, BUT, a bit of digging, can be rewarding. Living here has not turned up everything as other members have reported items not seen by me in the flesh.

Let us start with the North Bank.

Bus services in the Hull area in my time there were governed, or constrained by the terms of the July 1934 Co-ordination Agreement between Kingston-upon-Hull Corporation Transport and East Yorkshire Motor Services Ltd. The main provision was the division of Hull and its environs into two areas, known with the unimaginative titles of **A Area** and **B Area**, rather than the modern notation of Zones. This then lead to a sharing of revenues and costs, and the effective stifling of services by anyone else. The **A Area** was basically a ring drawn round the City close to the Tramway termini at 1934. (Some routes were subsequently shortened slightly so all the trams operated within the **A Area**, and one effect of the agreement was to be the death knell of the Tramway network). All revenues from this area passed to the Corporation. The **B Area** was the territory beyond this radiating outwards to include the first ring of satellite villages. Revenues less costs in this Area were shared. Parts of the **B Area** had previously been pure country territory, but when Hull extended its City Boundary in the 1920s problems arose. Corporation housing in Company territory. You do not need me to go over the details, it is a pattern repeated all over the Country, but dealt with differently in different parts. This coupled with the provisions of the 1930 Transport Act had profound effect on the services and tickets of the Hull area. Although Route Licences were jointly held within the co-ordination area, in practical terms most routes were operated exclusively by one company or the other, the exceptions being for mileage balancing purposes, usually early morning or late evening journeys. Post war housing developments were again shared out on a one company operating a route basis. In 1966, however, a new estate was built to accommodate slum clearance families. As there was only one estate this broke the established mould of sharing bus services and was a truly joint operation.

Colloquially pure EYMS territory beyond the **B Area** was known as the **C Area**, but this notation did not appear on tickets until as late as 1968, shortly before the agreement was re-negotiated, and the need for differentiating tickets was dispensed with. The revised agreement came into effect in December 1969 and aided the introduction of more automated fare collection systems.

This tying up of Hull left Connor and Graham of Easington the only local chink in the duopoly of Hull. West Yorkshire Road Car Co provided a little relief of red once every two hours on a joint service from Leeds. Lincolnshire Road Car crept in once a week with green buses, on a market day service from Scunthorpe, via Goole. In 1969, coincidentally after the renegotiation, West Riding Automobile Co, by now part of the NBC, began working some former EYMS journeys from Selby. South Yorkshire Road Transport tried a service to Manchester, but objections from the NBC and their developing National Express network, meant that although the coach ran through to Manchester, passengers wanting to travel through had to rebook at Pontefract. This obviously did not help and the service did not last long. More curious as the NBC did not provide a competing service! Of course, come 1986, the gloves came off! Kingston-upon-Hull City Transport as it had become known, took its eye off its core business. Private Hire, Low Cost Unit and Holidays were all tried, whereas East Yorkshire quietly consolidated its position with shrewd acquisitions of the post 1986 upstarts within the city. Connor & Graham just kept plodding on. The position at the time of writing is that Hull Corporation's descendent Stagecoach, is no longer the dominant local operator in the City.

EAST YORKSHIRE MOTOR SERVICES LTD

Based in Hull, EYMS was most famous for the shape of its double-decker buses. All normal height buses had a roof profile made to fit through a gated archway at Beverley, known as Beverley Bar. Even "new generation" lower floor buses in the 1960s needed a modified roof-line to be enable them to pass under this arch. A town centre bypass built in the late 1970s means this is no longer necessary as buses no longer pass through the arch. Many hours were spent at the Hull depôt chasing the high value **C Area** Willebrews

and Express Coach tickets, as this was really the only time you could obtain these as vehicles were being put to bed. The depôt staff were very helpful at the time, giving me my very own 'T-key' whilst still at school.

Willebrew

Less well known outside The Transport Ticket Society, is that EYMS was the last <u>major</u> company to hang on to the Willebrew ticket system. The Willebrew, whilst not reigning supreme at the end, survived until D-day in February 1971, with Returns being valid for a further three months. Apart from Ultimates on one route from 1966, no other machine saw service on Hull based services until after 1969 when the Agreement had been revised.

Because of the 1934 Agreement, three separate series of Willebrew tickets needed to be provided for Stage Carriage work. Further Willebrews existed for Express and Excursions. As with most Willebrew users, early tickets were wide, with title on the reverse. Later tickets were "normal" width.

In the **A Area** only one ticket was needed to cover all fare options. An early wide ticket shows **A Area** Returns, a Composite type with Single and Return fares on the same face.

In the **B Area**, an early wide ticket similarly shows

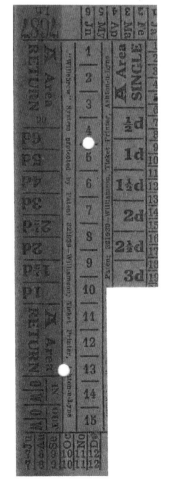

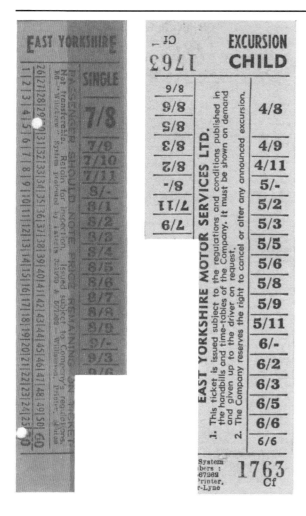

Returns, a Composite type with Single and Return fares on the same face. Later a ticket was provided with Single fares on one side and Return fares on the reverse, but as fares increased, it became necessary to provide two tickets, one for each of Single and Return.

In the **C Area** a range of Single and Return tickets were provided for, initially wide tickets as the other series. For conductors on routes starting or finishing in Hull and going to/from such exotic places as Scarborough, Leeds or Goole, tickets from all series were carried, making eleven in all. These tended to be in two racks, one for the Hull area tickets, which was dispatched to conductor's box when the **B Area** was left behind, and one for the rest of the route.

During the late 1960s subtle colour changes occurred to most values; e.g. **A Area** changing from mauve to pink, **B Area** became deep orange, and **C Area** tending to become deeper colours.

The only wide tickets I have personal experience with were those used for Excursions.

Ultimate

Ultimate tickets used by East Yorkshire fell into two distinct series. First was for Bridlington Town services

from 1952. Being a Williamson customer Williamson was the natural printer here. Tickets went through the normal development phases of large serials, small serials, normal paper, manilla paper, standardised format with the differing styles of value figure, etc. In fact quite unremarkable in their own way, but from a collecting point of view, and living in Hull, in the 1960s, a good reason to persuade the family to "Go to Brid" for a Sunday outing and get something other than Willebrew. Then in 1969, East Yorkshire changed printers and went to Bell Punch with Phase C style overprints and a new design.

As mentioned above, in 1966 a truly joint route was established with the Corporation Transport Department. This brought Ultimates into Hull. Unlike the Bridlington issues these tickets were a bit special. Still by Williamson and in standardised format, these tickets had overprints for **A Area** and **B Area** tickets, something the Corporation did not even achieve on its **A Area** Ultimate tickets, and something Williamson did not achieve on normal issue Ultimate tickets. These Ultimates were also printed with no grid because of the overprint, another feature not common with Williamson. The base ticket was in the style of the Bridlington issues. In 1969, one value was known to have become printed by Bell Punch, again in the Bridlington style with **B AREA** added under the title and Phase C style fare value overprint.

The Hull conductors did not like the Ultimate and the first sign of a jammed roll the machine was put away and Willebrews brought back into use as "Emergencies"!

The Ultimate was another D-day casualty with East Yorkshire.

Almex A

The Almex A had an intriguing gestation with East Yorkshire. Along with all operators, cost cutting exercises were prevalent during the 1960s. The two most obvious signs being service cuts and one man operation as it was called in those days, regardless of who was driving. East Yorkshire, however, had the problem of Hull's co-ordination area to contend with. Pure rural routes which stayed wholly within the **C Area**, moved towards Setright Speed machines (more

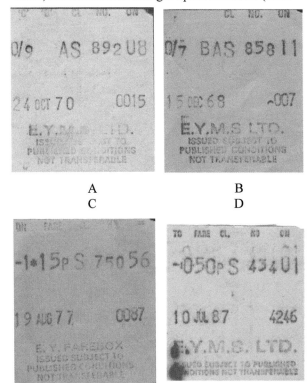

A   B
C   D

of which later). There was one rambling rural route from Hornsea on the coast, through Beverley and terminating at Hessle. Now, Hessle was in the **B Area**, so there was a need to record **B Area** revenue. (Not a problem with today's ETMs but not so easy with mechanical machines of the time). I am not aware of any trials with Setright Speeds of the type Mexborough and Swinton had, East Yorkshire went for Almex A with two sets of fare registers and for the first time **C Area** was noted on tickets (Tickets A and B). If a fare was issued in the **B Area**, a letter 'B' was additionally printed alongside the class (Ticket B). An absolute nightmare checking the Audit rolls! When the Co-ordination agreement was revised this distinction was no longer necessary and the 'C' and 'B' headings were removed form the printing plates.

Use of the Almex A then spread throughout the company gradually replacing all other types including Setright Speed. Machines were laid out differently to include route number. (Ticket D)

Hull Corporation was in the vanguard of introducing Autofare machines and associated Fareboxes, around the time of decimalisation, and East Yorkshire introduced Fareboxes on some of its routes within the City of Hull at around the same time. Unlike Hull though, no tickets were issued. Not surprisingly over-riding was rife as there was no way inspectors could

check on revenues. So in 1976, Almex As were coupled to these Fareboxes, but these machines were specific to Farebox routes and initially issued pink rolls to further highlight the difference from other Almex tickets. (Ticket C).

Setright Speed

Setright Speeds were introduced in 1958 on OMO services in the **C Area**. Consequently there was no requirement for apportionment of revenues under the 1934 Agreement. Machines were obtained from a number of sources with ex Westcliffe MS, Crosville MS and Northern General machines seeing service.

Some of these were converted for decimalisation in 1971. New decimal machines were also purchased. These new machines had machine numbers preceded by Δ. Some of these new machines were sold in 1981 to Conner & Graham, Easington, only to return when Connor & Graham was acquired in 1993.

Not surprisingly for a Willebrew user, rolls were supplied by Williamson, until about 1968 when NCR became the supplier. Cancellation grid for Returns was on the reverse.

Wayfarer

Mark 2 machines were introduced by May1987, replacing Almex A. Freedom brought about by deregulation in 1986 allowed the company to develop a strong branding. Ornate font and the Yorkshire Rose helped to develop this branding. Whilst outside the

[110mm x 37mm]

scope of the area under discussion, strong branding was developed in parallel in Scarborough, and this still exists. By the mid 1990s the brand was considered strong enough to be revised and tickets reflected this change. The introduction of Routemaster buses in Hull brought Clipper machines. Mark 3 machines with MCVs were brought into use by 1995.

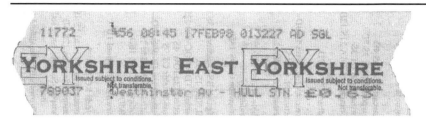

[145mm x 37mm]

[135mm x 37mm]

Advertising rolls generally had title on the front in a smaller font, regardless of whether the advertiser's logo appeared or not. Replaced by TGX150 machines by November 2001 in Scarborough and March 2002 over the rest of the network.

Wayfarer TGX150

Introduced in Scarborough by November 2001 and in the rest of the network in March 2002. The branding developed post deregulation has continued with TGX machines printing different titles in Scarborough and the rest of the network. Advertising rolls have had no effect on the front of these rolls.

Express Services

East Yorkshire operated Express Services on its own account and as a member of several pools. In my time the only acknowledgement of the pools was on luggage labels for luggage placed in the boot, although own title luggage labels also existed. Several evenings were spent obtaining these in my youth. Passenger tickets were of the style, which became the industry standard.

In addition to paper tickets for walk on bookings, East Yorkshire issued Willebrews.

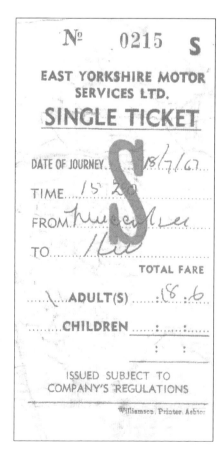

Magnetic Cards

East Yorkshire was involved in the Hull "Smart Buscard" scheme (more of which later), but outside Hull and in Scarborough, developed its own magnetic cards. Known simply as BUS/CARD. As with the flexibility offered with magnetic cards, several facilities were offered; 10 journey, point to point weeklies etc. Cards introduced in 1995 alongside Wayfarer 3s, were subjected to minor print revisions. Larger text for conditions statement and footer by 2000, and 1-10 cancellation punch holes added on reverse by 2001. Telephone numbers were also changed in 2001. Reverse of card issued on works service to BAE Systems at Brough. (More of this to come).

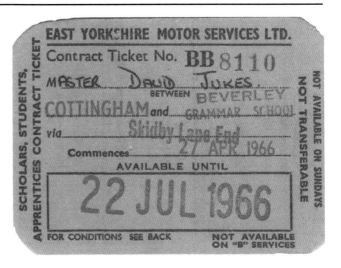

OTHER ISSUES

6 Saver

Following the introduction of Magnetic Cards with Wayfarer 3 by 1995, the North Hull group of routes, which were being operated by Routemasters, were unable to issue them. To compensate a discount card, known as 6 Saver was produced for this group of routes. Cards were available for Adult and OAPs. Said to be valid for 3 months, but tickets not actually dated on issue. Withdrawn in April 1995.

Contract Tickets

Contract tickets were provided of a design standard to the BET/Tilling group of the time. East Yorkshire must have had large stocks as a pink card was issued well into NBC days with the charge line of text on reverse still £ s d format. The constraints of the **A** and **B Areas** is apparent on the cards, but obviously not adhered to as Cottingham was in the **B Area**, (red card) and the route used to make this journey would be the Hornsea to Hessle service on which the special Almex As already referred to were used. Also of note is that the two cards issued to David Jukes, a friend of mine at the time represent his passage through his 18th birthday when still at school doing A-levels, i.e. no longer a Scholar, Student or Apprentice! (blue card). These were the days of course, when the local authorities who did not own their own bus operations, bought tickets from operating companies on behalf of Scholars who qualified for free travel.

In post deregulation times, things have changed and use of magnetic cards operated for a while, employer designated cards were produced (*Journal* 401/1988), the illustrated card here, and tokens for BAE at Brough.

Additionally in the 1990s school specific cards were produced, although I do not possess any myself.

Not surprisingly Williamson was supplier until replaced by a local printer, but not one of the obvious two!

Punch Tickets

And finally from East Yorkshire, some Punch tickets. Obviously I have no personal experience of Punch tickets being issued by East Yorkshire MS, but persistence in collector's shops finally delivered as recently as two to three years ago, and then again early 2007 from our Secretary Alan Peachey. I now can show only a very small selection of Punch tickets, non of which make reference to **A** or **B Areas**. It is felt on balance that there may not have been any so designated Punch tickets.

As they are Williamson prints note the mix of upper and lower case titles and serif and sans serif text. There is use of "and Associated Cos" in the title of some. Some independents acquired in the 1930s were not always fully absorbed on acquisition.

Left Luggage and Parcels Labels

Left Luggage and Parcels Labels of standard design were used in the days of large parcels networks. Two sets of rates existed due to joint workings. For parcels travelling north of Bridlington up to Scarborough or intermediate points, wherever the journey started, were subject to a higher minimum charge and a lower maximum weight, although within this narrower range, the poundage rates were the same. I am not aware of a different scale of charges for newspapers, and from my own experience of working in a shop, which was a parcels agent, newspapers we received had normal parcels labels on them, which is where the illustrated stamp came from.

MUNICIPAL TRANSPORT IN HULL

Kingston-upon-Hull Corporation, like many other municipalities, exercised their right to take over tramway operations from private operators, doing so in 1898. These were leased back to the Tramway operators until July 1899 when the Corporation took over full control. "Normal" development of services and the City took place in the early 20th Century, leading to the need for some sort agreement with the local company operator. This materialised in the July 1934 Co-ordination agreement with East Yorkshire Motor Services already mentioned. This, as with East Yorkshire, lead to the need for distinct series of tickets in this case two, until the agreement was renegotiated in December 1969. At deregulation in 1986, an arms length company, Kingston-upon-Hull City Transport Ltd was established. This company, now free of municipal constraints expanded into new areas which would lead to its downfall. Coaching was set up under the wholly owned company Kingstonian Travel Services Ltd, York Pullman Bus Company Ltd of Tadcaster was acquired and maintained as a separate unit in 1989, D. Coster (t/a Citilink), one of the post deregulation operators was acquired, and set up as a low cost unit to compete with all the other post 1986 operators. Citilink, York Pullman, Kingstonian were all registered as separate companies. Citilink and Kingstonian were wound up in March 1993 and York Pullman was sold on. The Company was then sold to a consortium of employees and Cleveland Transit Ltd in late 1993, passing to Stagecoach along with Cleveland in November 1994. Ownership stayed with Cleveland, but management facilities were provided by East Midland from Chesterfield. This was again altered in 2006 following the acquisition by Stagecoach of the Traction Group of Companies. Stagecoach in Hull operations are now managed from Lincoln, but legal ownership according to the vehicles, still lies with Cleveland Transit! When we get to this period of ownership, you will see this arrangement lead to Hull still going its own way under Stagecoach, until the introduction in 2007 of the corporate Wayfarer roll with self promotion advert on the reverse.

KINGSTON-UPON-HULL CORPORATION TRANSPORT

From 1934, Hull Corporation, like East Yorkshire, had to provide two series of tickets to account for the **A** and **B Areas**. This manifested itself on Punch tickets, and Ultimates. Staff at Hull Corporation's depôts were not as accommodating to a teenager as East Yorkshire, especially at the town centre depôt. This was the only depôt until 1970 to house vehicles fitted with Solomatics, and the depôt from which the Ferry buses operated. Let us just say a bit of trespassing and running was resorted to here.

Punch Tickets

I have no personal recollection of the use of Punch tickets by Hull Corporation but the post 1934 tickets are not difficult to come by. Pre 1934, tickets showed "Tramways" and then "Tramways and Buses." (The pre 1914 geographical issues have been documented

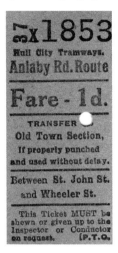

in Journal, some having **A Area** or **B Area** Journal). Post 1934, most had an **A** or **B** overprintin printed text as well. There were others still without overprint but **B Area** in the text. Titles were inconsistent, being H.C.T. or K.H.C.T.

Usually numerical stage, there were some "geographical issues.

Punch tickets were replaced by TIM on the Trolleybuses in 1949, and Ultimate on motorbuses in 1954.

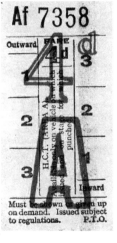

TIM

One reference source suggests TIM saw limited use on trams before the war. Dave Aspinwall's TIM reference work would tend to support this. As stated, all tram services after 1934 were in the **A** Area, so no revenue apportionment was necessary.

TIM machines were introduced in August 1946 on trolleybus services, there being no tram services left by then. The use of TIMs was again possible, as apart from one stop (for turning convenience), all trolleybus routes were within the **A Area**. Use of TIMs was fairly short lived, being replaced by Ultimate in December 1951. During Hull's days the machines were red inked. Tickets have been seen purple inked, but these are believed to have been issued by subsequent operators who bought the machines. My poor example comes from a machine which, curiously survived in the Conductor's Training School into the mid 1960s. An anonymous machine was used in 1966 for statistical purposes.

Ultimate

Introduced in 1951 on Trolleybuses and 1954 on Motorbuses. Initially, being used on Trolleybuses only one series, **A Area** tickets were required, and this remained the case on Trolleybuses until their demise in 1964. Motor bus crews, however, required **A** and **B Area** issues to cope with the requirements of the co-ordination agreement. With only 6 unit machines, this gave a limited range of values, and only three were available for each area. Some imaginative marrying was necessary especially in the **B Area** as fares increased. For example an 8d fare was not met with a double 4d, as the double 4d was used in combination with a single 4d to give a strip of three for a 1/-. Even then the strip of three was issued as a double + single, not the reverse. The 8d fare was met with a double 3d + single 2d. The 6d fare was issued as 2 x single 3d, thus facilitating cumbersome, but obtainable statistics.

Solomatic machines were used on omo services, and when manilla tickets arrived this led to two series of tickets running in parallel, normal paper being retained for Solomatics. Bell Punch remained the printer of Ultimates for normal services throughout. Tickets of both **A Area** and **B Area** followed Bell Punch's normal progression of print styles, including a "Tailored Issue" during 1959 printer's strike. Tickets overprinted "SPECIMEN" were used in the Conductor's Training School.

Panel headings reflected changes in facilities offered in the early days, with Returns only featuring on **B Area** tickets. Unlike punch tickets, **A Area** issues did not have any designating letter **A** printed. The designation letter was overprinted on **B Area** tickets until Bell Punch progressed to their Phase B and Phase C standardised printing (Society designations).

In this case the fare value was overprinted, consequently **B Area** tickets had a letter **B** pre-printed

with conditions offset to the right instead of the more usual central position as in the case of the **A Area** issues. At first the letter was large, reducing in size later. Following the amended agreement, **B Area** style tickets were dispensed with.

This finally allowed full use of the Ultimate machine's capability. However, an error appeared in 1970 when a 6d and later 3p were printed in what was now "the wrong colour" and more bizarrely, with a letter **B** in the text.

The march to 100% omo in the late 1960s/early 1970s lead to the replacement of Ultimates by Autoslot and, later Autofare equipment on normal services. Hull was the first major operator to achieve 100% omo as early as 1972. Ultimates, however, enjoyed an Indian Summer on special services to the docks for passenger ferries. These will be dealt with later.

Autoslot and Autofare

Autoslot equipment was fitted initially to double deck vehicles on omo services from September 1969. For passengers who did not have correct change, Solomatic machines remained in place. Machines were fitted in the luggage rack over the nearside front wheels, with later new deliveries being adapted to take the machines correctly. Fares were coarsened to permit the use of 3d or 6d coins only. Following successful operation of both equipment and omo double deckers (the staff were very enthusiastic and helped make it work!), joint work between KHCT and Bell Punch lead to the development of the Autofare System. Indeed Bell Punch publicity material of the day showed an installation on a Hull vehicle. The first Autofare installation was in November 1970.

The introduction of Autofare with fareboxes was not so enthusiastically accepted by the public, however, as an exact fare policy (the whole point of it), did not go down well with passengers not having the correct fare. The use of overpayment cards was not popular. Drivers were not permitted to give change, from their own pocket. This became OK for Hull residents, but for passengers arriving from New Holland on the Humber Ferry and catching the connecting service, many problems were encountered.

Tickets provided by Autoslot and Autofare machines by their very nature are not normally inspiring, with one ticket covering all fares. Hull did try and produced a range of issues over the years.

Trials with Autofare 3 were reported in 1985, but these were not adopted.

Other machines

Trials were undertaken with a Setright Speed capable of separating fares in two areas, like the Mexborough and Swinton Traction Co. Ltd., although in Hull it would not be necessary to show the split fare, simply register the fare on one or the other wheel. This occurred in December 1966 and January 1967. They were not adopted, as maybe the idea of a revised agreement was already afoot. The machine used was one of the batch numbered SETx, with the E printed backwards.

In early 1985, a group of services for wheelchair passengers and their companions was provided with funding from the City Council. A new Leyland National was bought with reduced seating and six wheelchair places. A "conductor" was carried to assist and was equipped with an Almex A. This was a former Rotherham Corporation machine with letters filed off leaving H (gap) C.T. on the cliché plate.

Also in 1985, Wayfarer 2 machines were introduced, but no titled rolls are known. Plain rolls, borrowed rolls from Grimsby Cleethorpes Transport and stock rolls were used. (Titled rolls did not appear until after Limited Company had been formed).

Ferry Services

Being a riverside city, the activities of Hull as a port could not escape the local transport system. There had been a long established service to the Eastern Docks for ship's crews, but this did not produce any special tickets. There was also a service to connect with the Railway Ferry from New Holland, and this too did not generate any special tickets.

The International Passenger Ferries, however, provided a completely different story. As might be expected, the fare carried a hefty surcharge when compared with the fare to the dock entrance by normal services. It was slightly higher than double initially, although as can be seen from the tickets, the fare remained stable as normal fares rose until it was rounded up quite a bit at decimalisation

Firstly they produced some of the few municipal bilingual tickets for other than commemorative reasons, in the U.K. Secondly, they had the fare in sterling and the currency of the country the vessel sailed from. Thirdly, bus drivers were able to accept this foreign currency; the Transport Department arranging with respective ship's pursers to exchange into sterling at a later date. Even Harold Wilson's devaluation of sterling had an effect on these tickets. Obtaining these tickets was not easy, as outbound passengers tended to hang on to them, thinking they may be needed to board ships. (Remember this was mid 1960s when International package holiday traffic was in its infancy). My father working for Customs and Excise at the time helped somewhat. Tickets were in the form of cards, with one for each service, making reference to the shipping line and which dock the sailing was from. (For those who do not know Hull too well, in the 1960s, Hull had nine separate docks connected to the

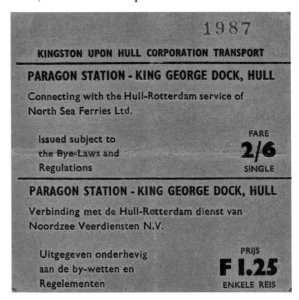

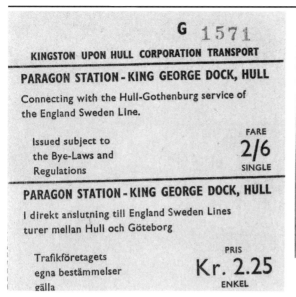

Humber through locks, a legacy in part of the pre-1923 railway companies desire to provide export facilities). Decimal issues have been easier to obtain, as these were replaced in 1971 by what must be the only bilingual UK Ultimates for normal usage. Decimal cards appeared readily at bus rallies in the mid 1970s.

England Sweden Line was a consortium of three shipping companies. In 1969, two of the companies, Svea Line and Swedish Lloyd withdrew form consortium leaving the Hull company Ellerman's Wilson Line to continue alone. This title change was also reflected on the tickets. Ticket colour was changed later from blue to pink.

At decimalisation of the UK currency, the alternative European currency was no longer printed on the ticket or accepted on the buses. The use of the title Associated Humber Lines was fossilised on the Alexandra Dock issue, as AHL had been wound up at the end of 1969.

The "AHL" service to Rotterdam ceased in December 1971; the EWL service to Gothenburg ceased in February 1972, leaving North Sea Ferries to reign

supreme. This company was subsequently taken over by P & O.

The Ultimates initially continued with a ticket for each ferry service, with initials of shipping line vertically printed. However, when two of the services ceased, a single, less attractive ticket was produced. In this case the fare was no longer printed, the fare being printed by means of the stage printer in the first position.

Services are still provided by P & O, successor to North Sea Ferries to Rotterdam and Zeebrugge. Normal Wayfarer tickets are issued today on the bus service, which no longer differentiates which ferry service, as there is only one trip each day for both vessels.

Although no special tickets are provided, the Scottish Citylink Service from Glasgow calls at King George Dock on its service to Hull for Ferry passengers.

Tours

City Tours were operated from 1951 to 1954 but I do not know details of tickets. Tours were re-introduced in 1975 operating Sundays from May until September. This time it was possible to partake in the tour only, or include an optional return crossing on the Humber Ferry and see the Humber Bridge under construction.

From 1981, however, this became a "Ride The Bridges Tour" and involved a City Tour crossing a major new bridge in the City Centre and the newly opened Humber Bridge. During the school summer holiday, this tour also operated three weekdays.

The opening of the Humber Bridge created new opportunities for the Transport Department, and Mystery Tours were set up involving a bridge crossing and finishing at Cleethorpes, Skegness or wherever. (East Yorkshire also provided similar tours but no special tickets). These were very popular at first and pre-booking was not required. When a bus was full,

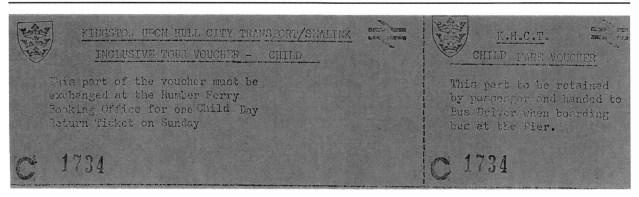

[210mm x 54mm]

KINGSTON UPON HULL CITY TRANSPORT/
SEALINK (U.K.) LTD., INCLUSIVE TOUR
6887
0923

Kingston upon Hull Circular Bus Tour

ADULT № 003357

Date 31 AUG 1980

Valid as Advertised

Issued subject to byelaws and regulations of
Kingston upon Hull Transport

Not Transferable

6887
KINGSTON UPON HULL CITY TRANSPORT/
SEALINK (U.K.) LTD., INCLUSIVE TOUR
0923

Hull (Corporation Pier)
to
New Holland and Back

ADULT № 003400

TOLL PAID   Date 31 AUG

Valid as Advertised

Issued subject to the regulations and conditions in the
publications and notices of the British Railways Board

Not Transferable

another one was simply brought round from the depôt and loaded. (Not sure where the drivers materialised from though, but often six or seven buses could be seen parked up in Cleethorpes.) Naturally as the novelty of crossing the bridge wore off, these tours declined.

Special tickets were provided, from specific issues in the early years to universal roll tickets by 1984.

Prepaids and Tokens

Prepaid tickets were provided for scholars in two age categories, under 14 and 14 to 16. I am not aware of any schools being open for normal tuition on Saturdays but prepaids were available for use up to 1pm on Saturdays. Maybe this was for sports matches representing the school? (I had other things to do like tickets to collect, than play sports). Over time, the

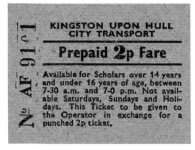

validity time from the start of the week of the prepaids changed from 8am to 7.30 am and this is reflected in the text.

Tokens were also provided for more general use, but a special for scholars 14 to 16 token existed. Why this distinction at the age of 14? Half fares were only available up the age of 14. Between the ages of 14 and 16 teenagers paid half fare plus ½d, not full adult fare.

When ½d fares were abolished, this principle continued, but rounded up to the nearest whole penny.

Crown Cards

This was the name given to a facility introduced in 1980, allowing unlimited travel over most of the network in Hull. East Yorkshire withdrew from the scheme at deregulation in 1986. Weekly and Monthly cards were provided for, in Adult and Senior Citizen options. A photocard was required.

First prints were narrow and horizontal like Cardiff and Portsmouth, but in 1984, "normal sized" portrait format cards became the norm. Card stocks meant use continued beyond deregulation and privatisation.

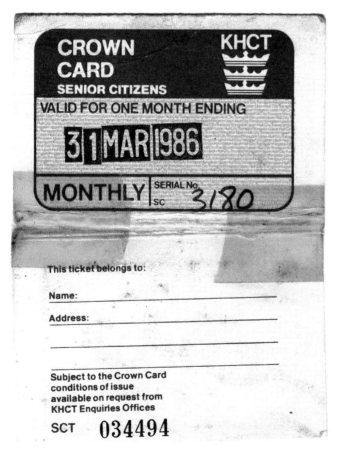

KINGSTON-UPON-HULL CITY TRANSPORT LTD

Following deregulation, the transport department passed to an arms length company with the above title. Given the freedoms this allowed, the fledgling company tried its hand at Private Hire, Tours etc under the Kingstonian brand. Two acquisitions were made, York Pullman and Citilink, which became the branding for a low cost unit Citilink, Kingstonian and York Pullman were all eventually registered as a companies in their own right. Their fate has already been mentioned. All this activity meant that the company took its eye off its core business, and serious inroads were made into the Hull scene by independents. The City Council then sold the business to a consortium comprising the company's employees and Cleveland Transit in December 1993. (Only the business and buses passed to this new company. The City Council having transferred the assets contained within and including the depôts to another department which leased them back to the Transport Department). This arrangement did not last long before Cleveland Transit sold out to Stagecoach Holdings in November 1994. The employees part of the consortium willingly accepted Stagecoach's offer to buy up the remaining shareholding. The company then adopted the Stagecoach way, and moved to new premises.

Tickets bearing the new company name were not plentiful, and although tickets existed with the subsidiary companies' names. I did not manage to obtain all of them.

Wayfarer

Wayfarer machines had been introduced shortly before deregulation, but as stated no titled tickets are known to me. This was not the case with the limited company who were keen to stamp their image on the local scene quickly. Publicity material at the time highlighted "the investment in Wayfarer machines means you will now be able to obtain change from the driver; there will no longer be the need to have the exact change"! A far cry from 1969/1970.

Equally, when Cleveland took over, it too was keen impress a new image shouting "EMPLOYEE OWNERS WORKING FOR YOU" from its buses and more importantly for us, from its tickets. This was not even sacrificed for logos on advertising rolls.

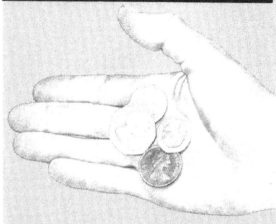

AVAILABLE SOON

K.H.C.T.'s new policy of giving change has got to be a change for the better! No need for the exact coinage, to fumble for the right coin and then wonder if you have given the correct money, because drivers will now have a change facility and there will be no need to worry about exact fares.

Of course, giving change can be time consuming and so we would like as many of our passengers as possible to have the correct fare anyway, but if you haven't the right money there is no longer any need to worry; the driver will make sure that's a change for the better!

And checking your ticket will be much easier too. We have invested in wayfarer microprocessor controlled ticket equipment, giving clear evidence of what you have paid and where you have boarded. Keep your ticket at all times.

[All these illustrations reduced by 20%]

Other Tickets

Not many other tickets have come to light from this period. Crown Cards continued to be issued, but are distinguishable from the Council company issues by virtue of the fact that "VALID FOR ONE WEEK/MONTH ENDING" was in a larger font size.

A last gasp from the Ultimate range for the Ferrybus appeared by 1993, still clinging on to its bi-lingual format, but, by now, incorrect title. A titled Emergency issue for use against Wayfarers was also produced.

STAGECOACH in HULL

During the 1990s as we all know, Stagecoach was a very predatory organisation. In late 1994 Cleveland Transit was acquired. It did not take long for Stagecoach to then buy out the employees part of the consortium which had owned Kingston-upon-Hull City Transport Ltd. A bit of defiant independence within the Stagecoach group was maintained in respect of their Wayfarer rolls until the introduction of the 2007 self advert roll! Advert rolls were "localised" as well. This may have been in part due to the complex ownership/management structure which exists in respect of Stagecoach in Hull. As with the Corporation many years ago, access to the current Stagecoach depôt is still difficult, but one thing I secured on retirement was an open dated permit from the Managing Director of the revamped Stagecoach East Midland Group in Lincoln, to visit any depôt within the East Midland Group. This is grudgingly accepted in Hull.

Wayfarer

Wayfarer machines were inherited and the design inherited initially was modified such that the "EMPLOYEE OWNERS WORKING FOR YOU" underscore to the title was amended quickly to "PART OF THE STAGECOACH GROUP". This modification appeared on the buses as well. When Stagecoach titled rolls eventually appeared by late 1995 (coincidentally in parallel with conversion to Mark 3 machines with MCVs), the roll was non standard, incorporating the KHCT title and phone number. The KHCT title was removed by 1997 but the phone number remained in place until 2007 when the self advert roll became the standard. Apart from advert rolls, it was not until 2006 that the "roundel" logo made an appearance on definitive rolls. Even this was not of the Stagecoach standard design, being a much larger font, "Thank You for Travelling" and Conditions statement running along the edge and still displaying phone number.

[145mm x 37mm]

[140mm x 37mm]

[135mm x 37mm]

Whilst these differences are not unique to Hull, the other operators within Stagecoach issuing non-standard designs until recently equally tend to be towards the end of long 'Cul de Sacs'! (Merseyside, South Wales).

Advertisement Rolls, however, eventually appeared to fall into line with corporate fronts, but still managed to arrange for local title and phone number to appear along the edge as late as 1999 before final submission in this area.

[115mm x 37mm]

[153mm x 37mm]

Ferry Tickets

In addition to being the death knell for Autofare equipment, Wayfarers finally saw off Ultimates. The service to King George Dock for P & O still runs, but passengers are simply issued with a Wayfarer. The only giveaway being route number and destination stage. This latter "detail" is only available on the outward journey as inward the stage is now Interchange (formerly Hull Station). This ticket is from a Day Trip my wife and I took to Amsterdam. The ferry crossing, plus bed, coach transfer, added to the bus fares from Cleethorpes to the dockside in Hull, was cheaper than a 'Ticket on Demand' day trip to London by train!

Magnetic Cards

Stagecoach in Hull was involved in the Hull "Be Smart" card scheme, (more of which later), but when this scheme was discontinued, developed their own card offering a range of facilities. By 2003, there was partial replacement by laminated wallets.

Laminated Wallets

Laminated Wallets appeared by 2003 for Megarider and Flexirider facilities.

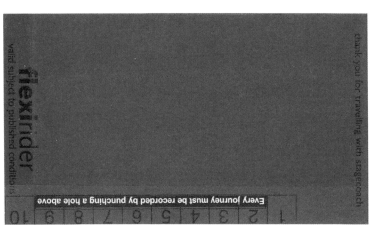

[125mm x 71mm]

The Other Stagecoach

Prior to (Sir) Brian Souter's Stagecoach becoming involved in Hull, the Stagecoach name was already in use.

Good News Travels was and still is a Christian Book shop in Hull. The company became involved in operating buses with pilgrimages to Lourdes, quite separate from The Across Trust. When the company decided to become engaged in stage carriage work by 1988, they adopted the trading name "Humber Stagecoach". The use of a horse-drawn stagecoach as a logo on buses and tickets followed. Stage Services passed to Pride of the Road, Royston in 1993. When Stagecoach acquired Hull City Transport Ltd in 1994, this company was still trading with vehicles carrying the Humber Stagecoach logo. This continued for some time, tickets, alas did not and untitled Almex As appeared. Good News Travels continued with Private Hire work until the crisis blew up in Roumania. The company then retreated back to its Christian roots and placed its buses at the disposal of humanitarian work.

[125mm x 70mm]

Hull Area's Other Independents

As previously outlined, the 1934 Co-ordination agreement and the effect of the 1930 Traffic Act effectively closed Hull to other operators.

The only notable exception being **Connor & Graham of Easington**. Operating by 1936, three services were provided from Easington, close to Spurn Point, to Hull by different routes. None were very frequent, serving mainly workers and shopping trips. Forces Leave Services were also provided for RAF Patrington. I have not seen tickets for this facility. The company did not use the City's main bus station, terminating adjacent to the Central Library, some five minutes walk away. There was interest in my days in the form of TIM, Almex A and Setright Speed machines, home produced 12 journey tickets and Contract Tickets.

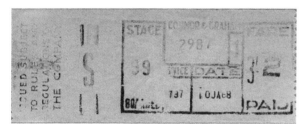

[97mm x 37.5mm]

[100mm x 37.5mm]

TIMs were replaced by Almex A in 1967, which were in turn replaced by Setright Speeds obtained from East Yorkshire by 1980. Connor & Graham sold out to East Yorkshire in 1994.

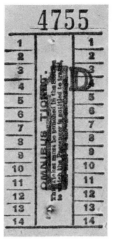

Before TIMs there were the well-known untitled Punch Period and Day tickets attributed to Harland, which have been distributed by The Society. However, a persistent visit to the depôt finally resulted in extracting a quantity of Harland (stock?) untitled single tickets.

Although an independent, the Contract Tickets followed the East Yorkshire style. Whether restrictions on picking up inbound and setting down on outbound journeys within the City existed, I do not know, but if there was no restriction, there was no reference to **A** and **B Areas** on issued tickets. 12 Journey Weeklies were home produced on a duplicator and a series of parcels tickets existed.

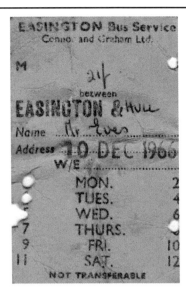

Deregulation

Following deregulation in 1986, things changed dramatically. Several operators tried their hand. As was usual elsewhere, services were operated only at profitable times with frequently changing timetables and routes. Anyway, collectively they rattled East Yorkshire and Kingston-upon-Hull City Transport Ltd. such that East Yorkshire acquired most of them in the period from the end of 1992 to 1994 and Kingston-upon-Hull City Transport Ltd acquired one. This did not see all of them off though. The Appleby Group from Conisholme (more later) continued until their demise through their own failings. Another attempt by independents was tried again in the early 2000s, but this time they lost out to stronger opposition from both East Yorkshire and Stagecoach. Universal use of Wayfarers issuing plain rolls! The only involvement by independents in stage carriage work except schools at the time of writing, is in the area of tendered services and one of the Park and Ride Service. However, as these are operated by Veolia (Alpha Coaches/Dunn Line), who knows what will happen in the future?

One completely new operator **D Coster (Citilink)** caused the greatest stir in 1988 using Routemaster buses in an attractive blue and silver livery and issuing horizontal punch style tickets. Despite several attempts, each time I visited I could only obtain the obligatory untitled stock ticket, in this case, Setright Speed. This was the company acquired by Kingston-upon-Hull City Transport Ltd. in 1989. Mr Coster was installed as a manager to run a low cost unit retaining the name Citilink. In this guise, the punch style tickets and Setright Speed continued, although the Setright Speed rolls gained a title on the reverse. Almex A eventually displaced Setright Speeds, but in 1990 and not as dated on the ticket itself. A Park and Ride service was secured, and horizontal punch style tickets were produced for this. This company was wound up in 1993 in preparation for the privatisation of Kingston-upon-Hull City Transport Ltd.

The Houghton's have been operating on and off since deregulation. Initially trading as Metro issuing plain Wayfarers and a titled weekly card, which I miserably failed to obtain one, although one has been illustrated in Journal. He sold his services to East Yorkshire in 1992. Private hire and schools work continued in a small way. He re-entered the fray in 1999 with licences in his wife's name, operating as **City Central**, with an orange and white livery, although some vehicles were painted in the complete former Kingston-upon-Hull Corporation Transport blue and white livery including City crest. The same enthusiasm was not extended to tickets, plain Wayfarers still being the order of the day. This period of operation lasted about three years. Schools services continued, getting a boost when the school contracts of **Amvale** were acquired when Amvale closed their Hull operation. Amvale had used titled broad roll tickets titled "Bluebird" and these continued in use. Unfortunately, when these ran out they were not replaced, the plain Wayfarers taking over again. In 2004 the company was renamed again to **Ellie Rose Travel** (Ellie Rose being the grand-daughter). A bit of enlightenment happened and the machines were titled to print Ellie Rose on the plain rolls. These are only on schools services as currently no stage carriage operations are undertaken.

A quite separate operations to these shenanigans was **Jowett Travel**. Operating from the same premises, this company was owned by Mrs Jowett, non other than the Houghton's daughter and mother of Ellie Rose. This company also ran some tendered services of its own in the 1990s, but used untitled Almex As. During the period of City Central, vehicles of both companies were painted in the same livery, Jowett then used Wayfarers issuing plain rolls. Jowett now operates private hire only.

The Bluebirds

I am aware of four quite separate companies in the Hull area using the name Bluebird, not counting the brief time with the Houghton's. The first one in the 1940s and 1950s were only involved in Private Hire and contract work, although they are represented by a preserved coach, a regular rally visitor until quite recently.

The second operator was based in Hessle and a former Taxi and Coach operator, **Mr Richardson**. This Bluebird entered the service field after deregulation with schools services and tendered services on the fringes of Hull to the west. Roll tickets were produced with a different roll for each day for the schools services. In July 1996, Mr Richardson disposed of the business to a P. Westfield.

P. Westfield continued to use the Bluebird name but from different premises and continued to produce a titled roll. This was now for a week, with colour rotation being applied. The rolls were broad with a coloured stripe down the centre and showing the address and phone number. They also represented only the second use of Harland to be reported in Journal for many years. (The first being Punch tickets for Green Bus, Warstone). Day tickets were different to Richardson's being narrow stock roll tickets with day and title hand-stamped on. Again several colours were used.

In 2001, P. Westfield sold out to **Amvale Ltd**, a Grimsby based operator who had previously been involved in schools and social services work.

Mr Westfield was retained by Amvale and moved to their operation South of the Humber. Amvale continued to use the Bluebird name on its school services tickets, but not its vehicles. It was already involved in a small way in stage carriage work, but like most other operators was using Wayfarers issuing plain rolls. Amvale's saving grace is that their's were pale green and not just white. A switch to Mark 3 saw machines programmed to print title on plain white rolls. On the schools services the broad rolls were retained and the hand-stamped narrow rolls were retained for day tickets. Under Amvale the company became a bit nomadic with regard to operating centre and fortunately these changes of address and phone number are reflected on the broad roll tickets. Expansion saw the acquisition of parts of the collapsing Appleby Empire, taking over some of the North Bank operations. The last move to Cottingham, however, proved their undoing. Despite taking over a former haulage depôt, complete with workshops, there were protests from local residents. Unfortunately for Amvale, there had been a period between the haulage company closing and Amvale moving in. The local residents complained about vehicle movements early morning and in the evening and eventually won an injunction banning such movements before 0800 and

```
AMVALE   11:52 19MAR TO 16:20 19MAR              020/£24.00

0206        DRIVER NO. 000010 DUTY 0157  B0182      ADL/SGL
```

after 1800 hours. Not very practical for a bus operation, and proving unworkable, Amvale closed the Hull operation down. Schools services were taken up by The Houghton's, who as shown earlier used up Bluebird rolls, but failed to continue the series. (Amvale still operates in the Grimsby area).

Alpha Coach Co (J.B. Porteous), had been a long established private hire operator who entered the battle in the early 1990s but was not successful and issued untitled or Yorkshire Traction titled Almex As. The Park and Ride service operated by Citilink was taken over, but the Almex As were used at first. The Handirider services previously operated by Kingston-upon-Hull City Transport Ltd were awarded in 1999, but again untitled tickets were issued, this time from Wayfarer 3, which had been introduced on another foray into stage services. Large numbers of school services are operated, although most of these are in the East Riding rather than Hull itself.

A little relief to the stock ticket scene occurred at Christmas 2000, when Alpha was alone in issuing Keith Edmondson "Merry Christmas" rolls. MCVs were fitted later and Alpha became part of the Hull Smart Card Scheme already referred to, but remained anonymous, issuing blank cards and their logo did not appear on the jointly titled card. Porteous, like Amvale, picked up bits of the collapsing Appleby Empire through an off the shelf facilitating company Seecroft Travel Ltd in 2001, but no Seecroft titled tickets are known to me, just the ubiquitous plain Wayfarer, and some Almex A90s. These were later re-programmed to print not only Alpha, but included reference to North Bank and Applebys, replacing Almex As on Park and Ride. Alpha passed to Dunn Line, and in 2006, invested in Wayfarer TGX150 machines shortly after the further take over by Veolia.

Veolia also operate a tendered service in the area to the west of Hull previously covered by Bluebird (Richardson).

In the above mention has been made of Applebys and Amvale Ltd. Both of these are companies based on the south bank of the River Humber and will be dealt with in more detail when we arrive there.

Hull Smart Buscard scheme

In a spirit of co-operation, but not of deregulation, some Hull operators combined to promote The Smart Buscard Scheme. Lead by East Yorkshire Motor Services and Stagecoach in Hull from 1995, Applebys and their associated company North Bank Travel and Porteus (Alpha Coach Co) were also involved at a later stage. All operators logos except Alpha eventually appeared on the cards. Serials tended to suggest which operator had actually issued the card, E for *EYMS*, K for *Stagecoach in Hull* and B for *Appleby Group*. Whether this was conclusively proved remains uncertain. Alpha issued blank stock cards.

Before we leave Hull, a reminder of pre-1934. **Binnington's of Willerby** was one of the companies based on the fringes of Hull, starting in 1885. The limited company was registered 8/10/1923. Services were Hull to Willerby and Hull to Hornsea. This company was acquired by East Yorkshire in 1932, although operated as a subsidiary until 1935. I obviously did not acquire these tickets from those days. These tickets were only acquired as recently as 2005 from a junk shop in Hull for a mere 50p each. They are out there if you care to look and be patient.

1996

Over the time that the scheme was running, the Stagecoach logo was updated at each print run, and Applebys and North Bank's logos were added. Changes in phone numbers are also noted ending up with the Hull Buscall number only. Despite all the changes to printed text, the print reference number, which did not appear on the initial print, remained the same subsequently. Independently of this scheme, EYMS had its own Magnetic Card scheme in Scarborough, and Applebys did in Lincoln. In both cases these cards were of a different design.

early 2001

1995

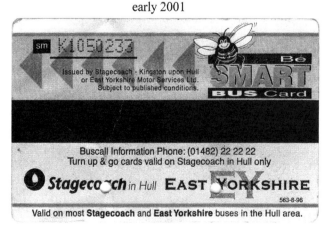

mid 2001

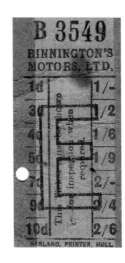

Cherry Coaches was main "user" of the works Travel Vouchers, which were somewhat geographical and offered single and return options in some cases.

The railways also provided facilities for the workers with weeklies from stations on the lines to Goole, Selby and Hull. These Edmondson types were over-stamped with week number as an added security measure. Tickets of the period illustrated would be sold at the works, and some do show Agent's number. Most of these stations were de-staffed in the early 1970s. Multiple Day returns were provided, not just 5 day.

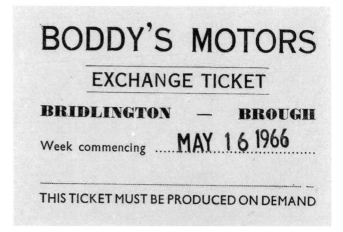

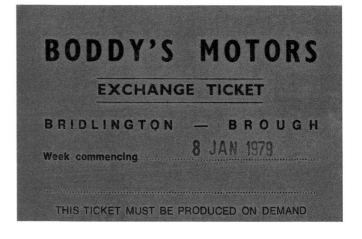

The Aircraft Factory

Proceeding west along the 'Cul de Sac' towards what some people would call civilisation, just outside Hull, at Brough there is a very busy aircraft factory. Now owned by BAE Systems, previous owners have been Hawker Siddeley Aviation Ltd and Blackburn Aircraft Ltd. Large numbers of works services were once provided by many operators. East Yorkshire even provided tokens for a period. There are still a limited number of services provided by East Yorkshire, but I am not aware of any special tickets nowadays.

Tickets in the past have been provided by operators themselves, and Travel Vouchers have been provided by the works. Workers are known to have come from Hull, Beverley, Bridlington, Market Weighton and probably Goole by bus and several points by rail. A selection of such tickets follows.

Boddy's Motors ran from Bridlington; **Cherry Coaches** from Beverley; **Ideal Motors** (J France) from Market Weighton and a Magnetic Card from **East Yorkshire**.

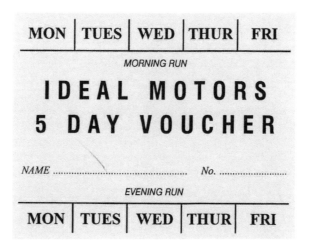

| MON | TUES | WED | THUR | FRI |

MORNING RUN

IDEAL MOTORS
5 DAY VOUCHER

NAME .... No. ....

EVENING RUN

| MON | TUES | WED | THUR | FRI |

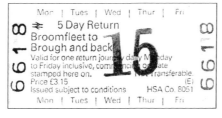

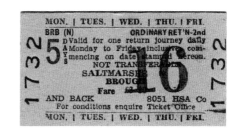

Holt's of Newport

Slightly further west was the village of Newport. This was the home of **J.A. Holt** (not to be confused with J.E. Holt of Reedness who still operates). J.A. Holt ran from Newport to Goole via the Marshes along the riverbank, the Hull service having been acquired by East Yorkshire in the 1930s. He issued Universal value tickets through the 1950s and 1960s. A 1984 depôt visit saw an Almex A audit roll, Ultimate machine and untitled Setright Speed ticket on the ground. A bit of overkill for one service! Mr Holt did not become involved in expansion following deregulation.

RAILWAYS

Hull was served by several railway companies, in the early years. The Hull & Barnsley Railway and its predecessors, the North Eastern Railway, and the Great Central Railway, being the main ones. Of these, the Great Central didn't actually run passenger trains into Hull. Their access to the City being "through the back door" by means of the ferry from New Holland. They did, however, have both passenger and goods stations in the City. The ferry will be dealt with later.

Discounting the Humber Ferry for now, the railway tickets I have been able to acquire are British Railways and later. Most are standard issues of the day so illustrations represent the less common bookings. Interesting amongst is the NCR 51 issued at Hull University Students Union, and an Exchange "to be handed to the Conductor of East Yorkshire Motor Services omnibus for a ticket". There was an interchange of tickets facility between East Yorkshire and the railways on the Hull to Bridlington line.

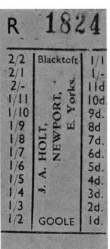

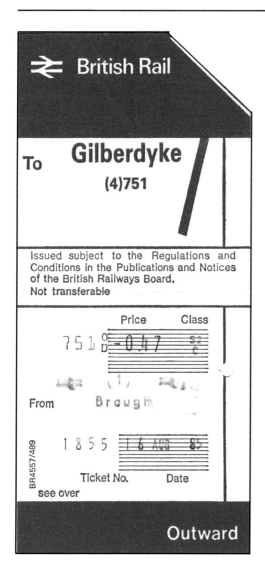

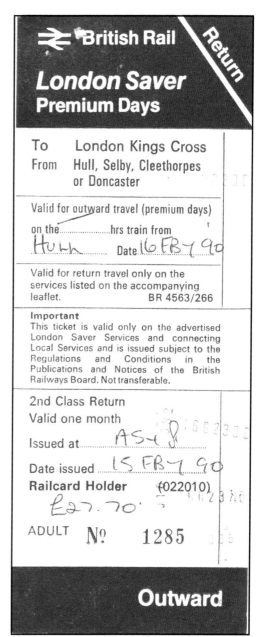

University stamp on reverse of the
above ticket

BOOTHFERRY PARK

Boothferry Park Station was built in 1951 on the "overhead" railway adjacent to Boothferry Park football ground, the then home of Hull City AFC, which was constructed in 1946. Being adjacent to the football ground, entry turnstiles were built directly from the railway station into the ground. (I believe the only football league ground to offer this facility). These were only used on the occasion of first team home games. When a connecting spur was built in 1962 to join the "overhead" to the main line into Hull from the west, it was possible to divert visiting supporters' trains to the ground (as well as its principal use for freight). This facility was not actually used very often, BR preferring to route visitors to Paragon Station, and charge them again to travel on the shuttle. Traffic was affected from the mid 1960s when KHCT began cross-city services to Boothferry Park from the North and East of the city.

This, coupled with increased car usage and a decline in fortunes of the football club itself, resulted in falling patronage and train service was withdrawn at the end of the 1985/86 season. I believe that technically the station is still open as there does not appear to have been the normal formal closure notice issued. This is somewhat academic as Hull City now play at the KC Stadium, on the site of a former Yorkshire Cricket Club ground, and have done since 2001. Boothferry Park football ground and platform still sort of stand, a haven for vandalism. Ultimatics were issued at Paragon Station for travel to the matches. For those not having tickets for journey from Boothferry Park after matches, Excesses were issued (or not) on arrival at Paragon.

CROSSING THE RIVER

The main reason two long 'Cul de Sacs' developed was the existence of the Humber Estuary to give it its correct title. Crossing this estuary had long been an adventure. The Romans walked across, a feat occasionally repeated for fund raising activities today. Ferry services slowly developed until the Manchester, Sheffield and Lincolnshire Railway (later Great Central Railway) established a significant crossing to gain access to Hull through "the back door". The service was developed from New Holland, which became a railway settlement and was an important location for the railway company. As well as the door to Hull, it was the eastern terminus of the railway until

it reached Grimsby and for sea traffic until it developed Immingham. Even one of the company's two laundries was at New Holland. There were proposals for a bridge in the 1890s but funding could not be raised together with the fact that many of the potential investors were shareholders in the Great Central and would not fund something which would affect that investment. The idea of bridging would not go away and in 1959 the Humber Bridge Board was established. The promise of a bridge came in a by-election in Hull in 1966. Construction started in 1972 to be open in 1976. Not surprisingly this was not achieved due to survey problems with the South Bank tower and the bridge eventually opened on 24 June 1981. It was the longest suspension bridge in the world at the time. The Ferry service ceased on the same day.

During 1969, a less well known service was started from Grimsby to Hull using small hovercraft run by a consortium of Grimsby businessmen. Unfortunately the vessels bought were too small for the degree of swell often experienced on the Humber and only lasted a few months. No tickets were issued.

The Ferry had been run by successive railway companies, passing to Associated Humber Lines in 1959. (AHL was owned by the British Transport Commission). AHL, which has already been mentioned in relation to European Ferries from Hull, went into liquidation in 1969, and management of the ferries passed to Sealink (UK) Ltd until it ceased.

As well as passengers and later vehicles, the ferries were used to transport produce from Lincolnshire farmers to Hull's fruit and vegetable market when the LNER withdrew its lighter services across the river. The barrows on which this produce was carried were subject to the same Toll Charge that was imposed on

passengers and motor vehicles for using Victoria Pier at Hull. Victoria Pier was built and owned by Hull Corporation and not the railway company. Conditions on the reverse referred to collection of toll "on behalf of Hull Corporation". Similarly when the ferries were

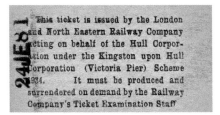

hired for sailings on Sundays or Saturday "Steamboat Stomps" as they were called, the Return Toll was payable.

A vast range of tickets existed for the ferry covering all sorts of vehicle lengths, two, three, four or more wheels; extra for trailer etc., passenger tickets to Hull and beyond from many stations south of the river, and from Hull to many locations southwards. Normal range of Single, Return, Privilege, Weeklies, Child were available. Naturally agency issues added to the range. Until 1969 when the Ferries became one class, there were upgrade tickets to saloon and foredeck.

A limited number of LNER Edmondson issues survived to the end.

When Paytrains were introduced in Lincolnshire in October 1970, pad tickets were carried by Guards for the ferry crossing, the Almex A ticket only covering journey to New Holland. Operationally during my use of the ferry, all south bank ticket issue was from New Holland Town station, even though all vehicle tickets are for journey from New Holland Pier. Passenger tickets were from New Holland Town.

The day after the ferry service ceased both New Holland Town and New Holland Pier stations were closed and a new station simply called New Holland opened. The terminus of the line became Barton-on-Humber, previously the end of a branch from New Holland Town. A new "interchange" was opened at the same time. Through journey bookings were still possible; a facility that was a casualty of bus deregulation. From stations with booking offices south of the river dedicated NCR51s were produced allowing onward travel from Barton on a (then) newly started bus service from Scunthorpe. The bus then went on to Hull's bus station adjacent to Paragon Station. In the reverse direction, the issued bus ticket allowed onward travel by train. The bus companies involved Monday to Saturday were Lincolnshire Road Car Co and East Yorkshire Motor Services. This hourly bus service still operates jointly by the bus companies. The train service from Cleethorpes also still operates Monday to Saturday, but two hourly. The timings still give a connection, but through bookings are no longer possible. Much reduced Sunday service from Scunthorpe keeps changing hands as tenders are awarded, and no trains run on a winter Sunday from

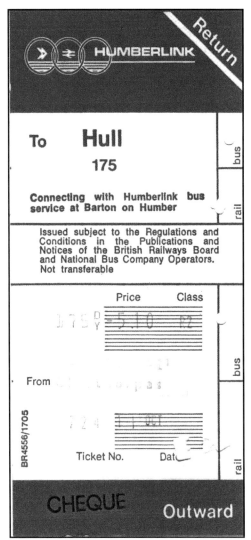

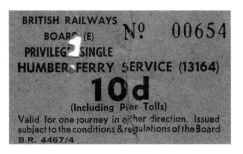

After audit, it was possible to purchase sets of all existing ticket stock from Hull Corporation Pier, for collections but sadly not from New Holland. This is where many in my collection came from, but some tickets were own use obtained with a bit of guile. My oldest son never got carried as much in his life except when travelling on railway facilities and I could not get tickets out of my pocket without upsetting him! It worked most times. A special ticket was produced for the Final Crossings.

The ferry was replaced by the Humber Bridge. Tickets are in the form of receipts or prepaids. Books of prepaid tickets come in 20s with a 10% discount. Each class of vehicle having a different colour, there are seven of them. Receipts for cash users were initially Almex Es with boasting text on the reverse. Nowadays pre-priced paper receipts are given with a hand stamp relating to which toll booth it was issued from. These stamps vary in font size.

Cleethorpes. This provision from Cleethorpes to Barton has been provided by a tendered bus service in previous years, but no one took up the mantle for winter 2007/2008.

Large numbers of tickets exist for all facilities cancelled with the last operating day of 24 June 1981.

BRITISH RAILWAYS BOARD (Z)

BOOK № 00072 TICKET No. 10/09

SINGLE JOURNEY

ONE PASSENGER (Toll Paid)

Between
HULL CORPORATION PIER
and
NEW HOLLAND PIER
Available in either direction

Not available after ....

CONDITIONS
Issued subject to the Conditions and Regulations in the
Board's Publications and Notices
NOT TRANSFERABLE

[159mm x 108mm]

[135mm x 74mm]

[135mm x 74mm]

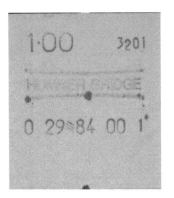

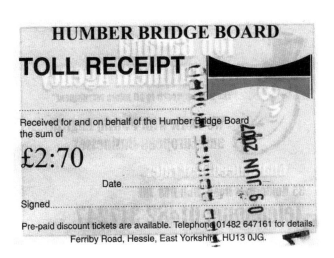

The vessels were available for hire on Saturday Evenings and Sundays. Saturday evenings were marketed as "Steamboat Stomps". This would be an occasion on which the Return Toll tickets would be issued. An attempt was made to preserve one of the vessels in the way that PS Waverley is. Alas, this did not happen, although the last three coal burning ships all survive as floating bars or heritage sites only. One on the Thames, one in Hartlepool and one in Grimsby.

Before returning to dry land, there are other ferries which ply the Humber, but these are for International journeys. During the 1960s there were three services already mentioned in connection with the bi-lingual ticket of Hull Corporation buses. One company now operates from Hull, P & O Ferries, to Europoort and Zeebrugge. There are overnight sailings to both destinations daily. Previously North Sea Ferries, P & O and Nedlloyd took over NSF in 1981. There has been a long but spasmodic history of international ferry services. The Great Central operated from New Holland and later Immingham. The LNER operated from Grimsby. Tor Line tried Immingham in the 1960s and 70s. And long distance services, to Australia, were provided by Ben Line up to the late 1960s. It was only really the advent of Ro-Ro services and the growth in package holidays that secured the present arrangement. DFDS-Tor Line re-commenced limited passenger traffic with sleeping berths on cargo ships to destinations in Europe in the early 21st century. Similar limited facilities are offered to the Far East from Goole

HUMBER PADDLE STEAMER GROUP

CRUISE TO GOOLE
aboard
P.S. LINCOLN CASTLE
(Weather and Circumstances Permitting)

Sunday 23rd. September 1973

Dep. New Holland	1340 Hrs.		Dep. Goole	1730 Hrs.
Dep. Hull Corp. Pier	1400 Hrs.		Arr New Holland	1940 Hrs.
Arr. Goole	1630 Hrs.		Arr. Hull Corp. Pier	2000 Hrs.

ADULT £1·60   With the co operation of **SEALINK**   CHILD 80p

[127mm x 92mm]

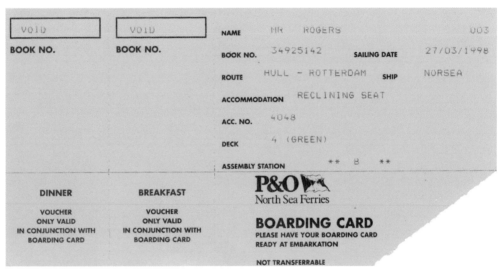

[197mm x 102mm]

[151mm x 82mm]

Round the River

Near the landward end of the 'Cul de Sacs' is Goole. This is a place one has to make a conscious decision to go to. The motorways naturally by-pass it. Prior to motorways, the main A roads in the area only skirted the edge when travelling from Hull to anywhere except the South bank. Consequently a visit to Goole was a deliberate act.

Bus services were not very frequent, but it was a meeting place. Holt's of Newport have already been mentioned. Lincolnshire Road Car ran in from Scunthorpe having taken over services from Yorks and Lincs and Ben Green of Swinefleet to add to their own operations. In fact it was Lincolnshire Road Car who had a depôt in Goole not East Yorkshire! From Doncaster, Blue Line (S. Morgan) provided a connection and West Riding Automobile Co Ltd crept in from Selby. The advent of the NBC, South Yorkshire PTE and falling patronage in the 1970s was to change all this. Scunthorpe is now served by another Holt (Sweyne Coaches), this time of Reedness, but with tendered services. East Yorkshire still run in. Local town services keep changing hands as the re-tendering process grinds on. East Yorkshire, Mainline, First Group taking it in turns. Doncaster was accessed by First or Leon of Finningley. The current Goole based operator, Drury (Blenheim) serves outlying villages and schools north of the river, but in keeping with this territory issues blank Setright Speeds.

The big companies issued their normal tickets, but the independents made the trips to Goole worth while. Ben Green and Yorks and Lincs issued Punch tickets, Holt Newport issued the Universal tickets already mentioned until giving in to stock items, Blue Line issued Willebrews, which unlike East Yorkshire generated one of the few decimal versions of this ticket system, later replaced by TIM.

Of the current crop, Holt of Reedness issues Wayfarer with plain rolls, but operator identity in machine printed data. Leon of Finningley/MASS Transit issued Almex A90, without operator title, but a series of advertisements for their holidays and tours.

32

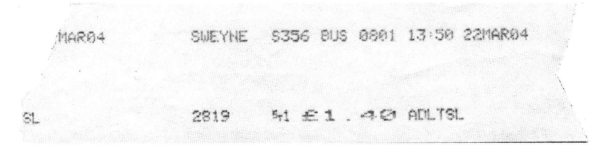

South Bank Buses

Having travelled round the river, we pass over the bleak marshes of the Isle of Axholme to Scunthorpe. A large presence by Lincolnshire Road Car (t/a Stagecoach in Lincolnshire) dominates the town, but there has always been a presence by independents. Mostly issuing stock or untitled tickets in my visits, Hornsby eventually caused a stir back in 1994 by producing a titled Setright Speed roll. Although this roll still sees limited use on schools services, normal services saw the introduction of Almex A90s in 1996 and even magnetic cards in 1997. To back track though, Lincolnshire Road Car (formerly Enterprise &

Silver Dawn, before my time!), Hornsby, Millard (Ubique), of Scawby and Hankin of Scunthorpe operated jointly from Scunthorpe to Ashby. I never saw any of Hankin's buses, they having ceased by the time I was visiting Scunthorpe, but Millard proved to be worth digging out. He only operated obscure journeys as his share, but unlike Hornsby, did have titled tickets; Almex A in my case.

Post deregulation only Lincolnshire and Hornsby were left. A jointly titled card appeared but I did not capture one. Later competition seemed to take over

from co-operation, and when Stagecoach acquired Lincolnshire Road Car (as part of the Yorkshire Traction Group), Hornsby introduced a weekly laminated wallet in response to Stagecoach's Megarider. The card was not titled itself, but is easily identifiable even without a ticket inserted as Hornsby's. The other sizeable operator in Scunthorpe, Holloways Coaches, only has a small presence in stage carriage work. They operate many of the school contracts in and around Scunthorpe and Brigg and free shoppers services. Despite all this activity, untitled Almex As are used.

To Cleethorpes.

I moved to Cleethorpes in April 1969. The effects of the "Cod Wars" with Iceland meant there was little work in Hull at the time I left school. The trawling fleet was grounded, not that I had intended going to sea, but all the shore based support industries were closing, resulting in a high (for that time) labour surplus. On the other hand, South of the river, despite a similar situation occurring with the Grimsby fishing

fleet, there were alternative developments and expansion in the vegetable processing industry and petrochemical industry. Land was cheap and labour was short. Hence the move.

The day I moved involved a ferry crossing and train journey. My first sight of buses in Cleethorpes was Peter Sheffield Coaches, who parked much of their fleet on the car park next to Cleethorpes station. Despite a fleet of over 40 vehicles, no services were operated. I felt disappointed. Later I was to find out that they had operated a service for about two years using bar titled Setright Speeds. But this was before my time. Other tickets did eventually appear for their tours and holiday programmes. In the 1980s the phenomenon of concert tours commenced, and Peter Sheffield Concert Tours was set up. This was a separate company in which Peter Sheffield was a partner. Tickets were produced for these. Peter Sheffield eventually sold out to Grimsby Cleethorpes Transport Company Ltd in 1988. Although run as a separate entity including in Stagecoach days, no pre-printed titled tickets are known to me.

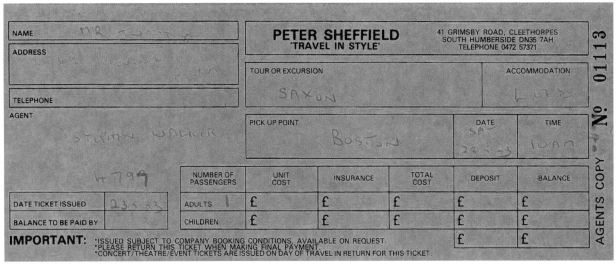

[190mm x 75mm]

[190mm x 75mm]

There was hope with the commencement of Stagecoach Express 909, in 1994. This was initially licensed to Stagecoach Peter Sheffield, running from Cleethorpes to Doncaster, but standard Stagecoach Grimsby Cleethorpes Transport Wayfarers were issued. Service 909 was remarketed in July1995. Now running from Grimsby to Meadowhall and Sheffield, with a link to Hull, and serving Humberside Airport. A titled Stagecoach express roll appeared for this rebranding, although a different design from the Scottish roll with the same title. Operations were now in the hands of Stagecoach Grimsby Cleethorpes, Stagecoach East Midlands and Stagecoach in Hull. Three vehicles met south of the Humber for passengers to transfer between vehicles. The service was hourly from 0600 until 2000. Very popular initially and duplicates were frequent on early morning departures from Grimsby. A deal with GNER from mid 1997 allowed through booking from Service 909 to London Kings Cross for £20! by specified trains. A

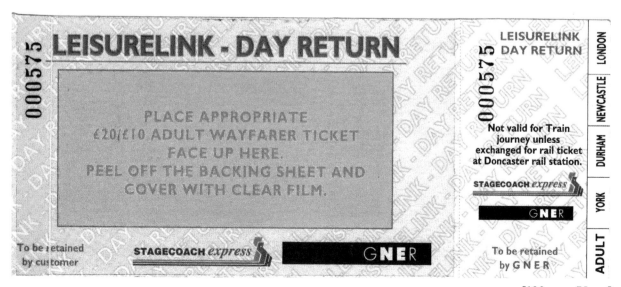

[180mm x 75mm]

laminated wallet titled Capitalink was produced for this, with detachable voucher to exchange for rail tickets.

Due to its initial popularity, north bound connections to York and Newcastle were offered for a while and the facility was rebranded Leisurelink. This facility was reduced when bus service was reduced. The facility was eventually withdrawn by mid 2000. The bus service is now a shadow of its former self and only runs from Cleethorpes to Hull, although still hourly but with no evening journeys. No special tickets exist today, although ticket issue is currently Stagecoach in Lincolnshire Almex A90. In its heyday, a wallet was produced for students, which when bought gave a third discount.

Applebys a long established company based at Conisholme in Lincolnshire should be well known as another user of stock tickets when they introduced Setright Speeds, some of which saw nearly fifty years service! They became involved north of the river, with the acquisition of Boddy Motors of Hull and Bridlington in 1982 and 1983 respectively. (Further operations, outside the scope of this talk, were set up in Scarborough post deregulation). In Hull, a coach company, Halcyon Travel was acquired in 1993, but retained as a separate operation. Under Applebys own name several schools contracts were added in 1997. And in 1998, Fleetjet (t/a North Bank Travel) was acquired as a low cost unit, retaining its own identity. The Appleby operation got too big, stretching from south of Lincoln to Scarborough. It began to creek round the edges starting with the Traffic Commisioners closing Scarborough for failing maintainance. The dominoes just started to fall until the whole Empire collapsed in 2001 on the north bank and 2002 on the South bank. Unlike the South bank, some titled machines appeared in Hull and beyond (and Ultimates in Lincoln); Almex A, Almex A90 and in Bridlington Wayfarers issuing plain rolls with machine I/D BRID 02 etc. Whilst expanding north of the river and in Lincoln following acquisition of

Hudson's of Horncastle, there was little movement on their home ground. Services around Grimsby remained unchanged as a direct result of deregulation of stage services and the untitled Setrights plodded on.

Not so with deregulation of Express services in 1980. In this case, a service was inaugurated under the Poacher branding to Kings Cross. This was from Grimsby through Lincoln, but was not well patronised and was an early casualty of the false optimism at that time. In the background, a programme of day trips and holiday tours was operated. Titled receipts were issued for payments to these offerings. The low cost unit in Hull issued untitled Almex As and the holiday company Halcyon Travel provided me with a luggage labels only.

Like Peter Sheffield, Applebys became involved in concert tour work, but in their case only as a contractor to Solid Entertainments of Grimsby. This ticket, though bearing Applebys name, is not one of their own issues.

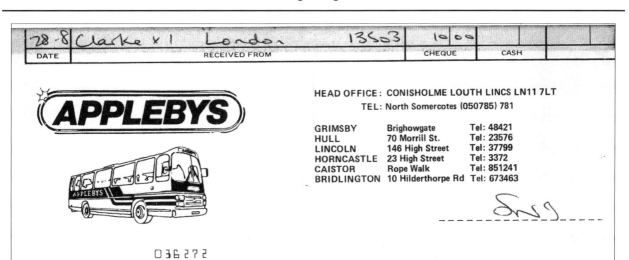

DATE	RECEIVED FROM	CHEQUE	CASH	
28-8	Clarke x 1 London	13503	10 00	

[214mm x 82mm]

[175mm x 76mm]

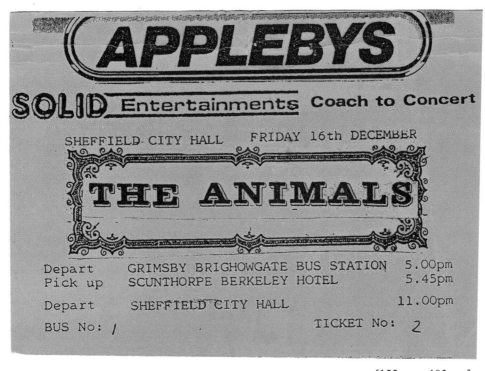

[152mm x 103mm]

```
      SINGLE
  CHILD  £00.25
  From:  11 GOUT'S BR
  To  :  12 LIBRARY
  F0025 Rt  1D D 542 B 740
  18-Jun-99 Tck:6150  15:43
      APPLEBYS
      of LINCOLN
    tel: (01522) 537799
```

HOMEWARD

Name..

Address.......................................

....

HALCYON TRAVEL

[88mm x 60mm]

RETURN E 100686

APPLEBYS COACHES
LUXURY TRAVEL
Conisholme — Louth — Lincolnshire Tel. (050785) 361

SERVICE OPERATED BY			
SINGLE DAY RETURN PERIOD RETURN			
TO	CLEETHORPES Market Place		
FROM	LINCOLN		

OUTWARD Service No. or Coach No.	DAY Saturday 07	DATE 03 1981	TIME 0650

DATE OF ISSUE 05 03 81 One	No. of Passengers ADULTS 3-00	Fare Each	£ TOTAL p 3 00
AGENCY No. G7	CHILDREN		.
ISSUED BY J07			.
BOOKING REF OR SEAT No.	OUTWARD	RETURN	TOTAL FARE 3 00

RETURN Service No. or Coach No.	DAY Saturday 01	DATE 03 1981	TIME 2145

BOARDING AT LINCOLN.

PASSENGER'S NAME AND ADDRESS
Mr SALT, 90, BARCROFT ST, CLEETHORPES

ADULTS 1	CHILDREN	TOTAL FARE £ 3 .00

This ticket is issued subject to the Conditions printed overleaf and to the Conditions set out in the OPERATING COMPANY'S Handbills and Time-tables.   E 100686

[100mm x 154mm]

Amvale Ltd are based in Grimsby and had been involved in Social Services work. They picked up some bits of Applebys demise in Hull, mainly bits of North Bank Travel, but as shown with Alpha not all of it. Also picked up were the South Bank operations, except the touring division, which had already passed to the Bowen group. Ticket wise, Amvale also picked up Applebys untitled Setright Speeds, Almex As and Wayfarers. Titled tickets do exist in the form of Tours and Scholars.

Before looking at the major operators in the Cleethorpes area, there was one other company involved in stage work, **Granville Tours** of Grimsby. This came courtesy of **Starks of Tetney**, acquired in 1964. Stock tickets were once again encountered, this time Bellgraphics. An express service was operated to Great Yarmouth on summer Saturdays and this with Excursions and Day Trips did, however, generate some nice titled tickets. Granville Tours got caught up in the problems of Zebra holidays and closed down in 1983. Although Starks had ceased PSV operation in 1964, he continued in haulage until the early 1990s. When his premises were being sold for redevelopment as housing, a visit winkled out this nice excursion ticket from a cupboard! Some of Stark's punch tickets were distributed many years ago.

To round off Applebys, the Lincoln, Bardney and Horncastle operations went to ITG, South Anston. Holidays and Tours went to Bowen's. However, Mr Appleby did not lie down. He was appointed by **Cooper's of Killamarsh**, a company that had provided feeder coaches for Applebys holidays from South Yorkshire and Derbyshire in the past. Like a phoenix, the Appleby name was resurrected for an open top service in Cleethorpes, taking on Stagecoach. True to form, untitled Wayfarers were issued, but they were at least on gold rolls and for one season had the name Appleby condensed to six letters. A jointly titled ticket was produced for tours. Problems arose using the Appleby name, as this was and still is in use by the Bowen Group for holidays and tours, and the Appleby name was quietly dropped by Coopers. In 2007, the open toppers still operate along Cleethorpes seafront in competition with Stagecoach!

Amvale
coaches

Travel Pass (Fare Paid)

Name: **Miss. Julie Broderick**

Authorised by:

Valid From: 01/09/06 to 24/12/06
Tel: (01472) 355600
Cherry Park to Grimsby & Return (One Return Journey per Day)

[101mm x 67mm - before lamination]

AMVALE LTD
Of Grimsby

COACH EXCURSION

FROM BOARDING AT			
TO			

DAY	DATE	TIME	
		OUTWARD	RETURN

			TOTAL	
			£	p
Adults @				•
Children @				•

AGENCY No.	DATE OF ISSUE	TOTAL FARE		•

PASSENGERS NAME & ADDRESS

A 15604
Ticket Issued subject to Conditions of Booking | TEL No.

[104mm x 147mm]

DATE	DESTINATION	ADULT	CHILD	TIME OF DEPARTURE	AMOUNT PAID
15/8	MKT RASEN	3	2	1.00pm	6.50

Kalamazoo 629949-1¾x6½

GRANVILLE TOURS

FROM: **BRIGHOWGATE BUS STATION**   EXCURSION TICKET NO.

ALL EXCURSIONS WILL BE OPERATED SUBJECT TO SUFFICIENT SEATS BEING BOOKED. THE COMPANY RESERVES THE RIGHT TO CANCEL ANY EXCURSION WITHOUT PRIOR NOTICE.

07638

HEAD OFFICE: **NORFOLK HOUSE, WELHOLME ROAD, GRIMSBY**   PHONE 55031

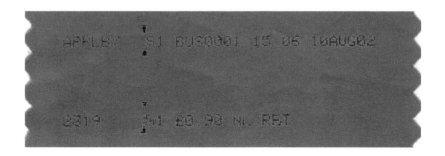

Granville Tours ticket

OUTWARD JOURNEY
CAX
A 2305

GRANVILLE TOURS
LIMITED
"Norfolk House," Welholme Road, GRIMSBY
FOR CONDITIONS OF ISSUE SEE OVER

SERVICE **54**

DELETE AS NECESSARY | SINGLE | DAY RETURN | PERIOD RETURN

BOARDING AT **GRIMSBY (Bus Stn.)**
ALIGHTING AT **Gt. YARMOUTH (BEACH COA**

	Date	Time
OUTWARD JOURNEY	6.6.81	08.00
RETURN JOURNEY	13.6.81	15.00

Number of Passengers		FARE EACH	
ADULTS	1	£9.00	9.00
CHILDREN			

Date of Issue	Initials	Agency No.	TOTAL FARE	
11.2.81	DS	FTC		9.00

NAME **MR. BANTON**
ADDRESS **12 COLE RD. CLEETHORPES**

THIS PORTION TO BE RETAINED BY PASSENGER

ADULTS	CHILDREN	TOTAL FARE PAID	
1			9.00

FROM **GRIMSBY** TO **YARMOUTH**

OUTWARD DATE	6.6.81	RETURN DATE	13.6.81

A 2305

[95mm x 157mm]

Appleby Coaches / Coopers Tours ticket

APPLEBY COACHES Ltd.
& COOPERS TOURS Ltd.

DAY TOUR AND THEATRE EXCURSION TICKET

Excursion		No. 1939

Excursion Day & Date				Reserved Seat Number		

Boarding Point(s)				Time(s)	

Lead Name: (for correspondent) Mr/Mrs/Miss	Initials:	Surname:	Passenger Names (including lead name)	Price Per Person	Adult OAP Child
Address:				£	
				£	
				£	
				£	
Postcode:			Total Excursion Price	£	
Home Tel. No.:			Payment made by Cash/Cheque/D. Card		

Date of Booking		Credit Cards Credit Card Bookings are charged at £1.25 per £50 value or part there of	Please see our current Brochure or Leaflet for our Booking and Cancellation details.
Agents Stamp			**Appleby Coaches Limited** 24a, South St. Mary's Gate, Grimsby, North East Lincolnshire, DN31 1LQ. Telephone: 01472 353544
			Coopers Tours Limited Aldred Close, Norwood Industrial Estate, Killamarsh, Sheffield, S21 2JH. Telephone: 0114 248 2859
Agents Ref.			

Great Days Out for Family and Friends

[149mm x 199mm]

Stark's Luxury Coaches ticket

№ 2443

Stark's Luxury Coaches

F. A. STARK & SON, Tetney, Grimsby and Cleethorpes
'Phone: Humberston 2183

All Tours commence from Cleethorpes Market Place.

Extended Tours to .... Days ....

Date of depart .... Time ....

No of Passengers			£	s.	d.
Adults	Children	Deposit Paid			
		Balance to pay			
Seat No's		Total Fare			

LUGGAGE—
One suitcase per person, approximately 36" x 15"

BOOKING AGENT
16 MARKET PLA(
CLEETHORPES.

Conditions—
We do not undertake that the Cars shall start or arrive at the times specified, nor will we be accountable for any loss, inconvenience or injury which may arise from delay or detention.

Issued subject to the terms and conditions outlined in our Brochure.

[143mm x 120mm]

Major operators on the South Bank

In 1969, Cleethorpes and Grimsby were to be further disappointing as well as Peter Sheffield having no services, the two major operators could only offer Setright Speed or TIM. Having been brought up in Hull's restricted, but interesting environment, this was positively boring.

Lincolnshire Road Car did have some residual use of Insert Setrights, but not in Grimsby. There was not a coordination agreement operating in the way of Hull. The company and municipal operations had gone their own way until the cut backs of the Grimsby and Immingham Tramway by British Rail. A joint service was inaugurated in September 1959. The terms were not, however, straight forward. A point on the then boundary of Grimsby is called Toothill. From Cleethorpes to Toothill, Grimsby Cleethorpes Transport fare scales applied, and from Toothill to Immingham Dock, Lincolnshire Road Car fare scales applied. The most obvious difference being in respect of child fares, which were half on GCT scales and two thirds on Road Car scales. This situation continued until deregulation. In the 1960's a new residential development The Willows, was established along the road from Toothill and from the start this was registered as a joint service. Again following deregulation, GCT was left to operate this on its own. Unlike Hull, all revenues and costs remained with the operating company. All other Lincolnshire routes into Grimsby and Cleethorpes charged pure Road Car fares, expensive by comparison as there was no municipal subsidy.

Shortly after deregulation, Lincolnshire Road Car overstretched itself elsewhere and closed down it's Grimsby operation, including some newly registered local routes around Cleethorpes. Having sorted out Scunthorpe, Skegness and most notably Newark, Road Car returned to Grimsby in 1988 to take on GCT (the depôt had not been sold, being used for vehicle storage).

Lincolnshire Road Car was to say the least, very conservative in its ticket issuing systems in the time I have known it. Setright Speed, replaced by Almex A in 1986, and Almex A90 in 1993. When taken over by Stagecoach in 2005, it became notable in that it was the only Stagecoach company using the A90 system. It still took 18 months, however, to re-programme the machines to read Stagecoach Lincolnshire.

The introduction of attractive advertising rolls by Brittannia although nothing to do with Road Car directly, did brighten up the scene, including some of

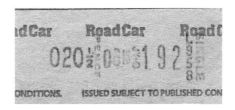

the few Almex A varieties produced nationwide. The Almex A90, along with other users, managed to have the title printed on the reverse **with** the advert rather than the Wayfarer way of printing the advertisers logo on the front.

On its return to Grimsby in 1988, there was a bit of a skirmish between Road Car and GCT, but Road Car had lost the initiative regarding Immingham and left well alone. It did try to cream off day time traffic from two estates plus the former Willows route. Mini buses, all the rage at the time flooded the streets from both companies. Common sense quickly prevailed and Road Car withdrew most of its competing operations. The service to the Willows did remain, but with both companies alternating on a 15 minute frequency. This was not a joint service as it had been previously; it survived in this form until the Stagecoach takeover, and is now wholly licensed to Stagecoach Grimsby Cleethorpes. The Road Car did produce some 10 and later 12 journey tickets for this route. Road Runner was the branding given to the minibus operation. The 12 journey wallet was short lived as the printed text disappeared as we all know.

Although these had been withdrawn by the time I started driving for the Road Car, arguments on the platform were commonplace due to the differing fares between the two operators from certain points required under competition rules. The passengers could not or would not understand this.

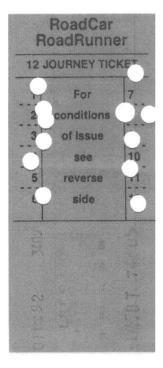

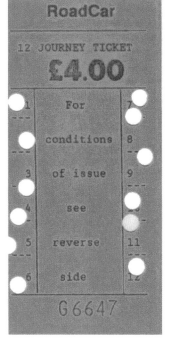

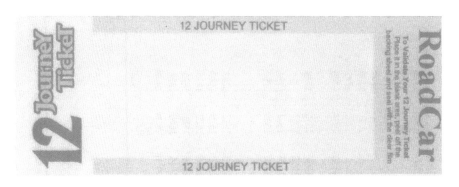

[170mm x 61mm]

Working for Road Car from 2001, opened doors to tickets I was unaware of. A problem existed on vehicles working into Lincoln from other depôts. In Lincoln, magnetic cards were used for 12 journey, weekly and monthly tickets. Vehicles from other depôts were not equipped with MCVs. Passengers boarding with magnetic cards were recorded on the Almex A90 using the return cancelling punch, 12 journey cards being punched. A passenger boarding requiring a 12 journey received a long strip from the A90, which was not placed in a wallet. (This tidy example came from the training school). It was not possible, however, to issue a weekly ticket. This was addressed in 2004 with the introduction of a laminated wallet, branded Pogo (jump on and off!). In 2005, a directive was issued that ALL drivers would issue Pogos to avoid passenger confusion, and the ability to issue weeklies through MCVs was deleted from the software of Lincoln driver's machines. It should be noted that due to limited storage capacity, the data stored in the A90s and drivers ACE, was depôt specific, and an ACE from the "Wrong Depôt" scrambled the data and rendering the machine and ACE requiring reformatting.

A selection of other miscellaneous tickets follows. A non Lincoln monthly issued manually at depôts; complimentary for passenger complaints, staff passes and a good looking fella!;

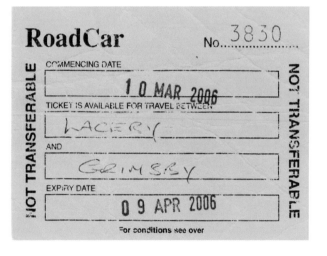

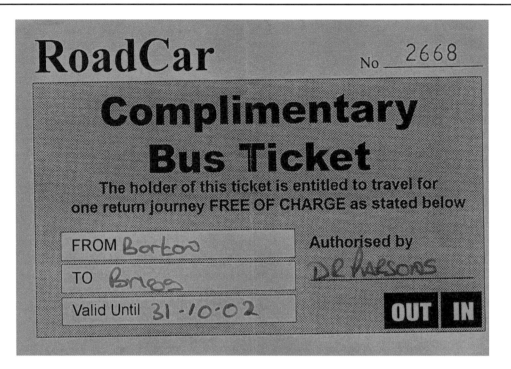

Emergencies and Transfer of Passengers Voucher. This last item was accepted on Grimsby Cleethorpes Transport joint route at Immingham on the one trip where a Road Car service from Scunthorpe met a GCT working for passengers who had paid for onward travel.

In December 2005, Road Car, as part of the Yorkshire Traction Group was acquired by Stagecoach. A shaky start due to competition worries in Grimsby, the all clear was given in April 2006, Stagecoach Megarider titled laminated wallets appeared within days. Two versions were to be found. One with and one without reference to "Road Car." In 2007, an orange wavy line was added to front.

Almex A90s were not re-programmed until September 2007 though. In Grimsby, the Road Car operation was moved into the Stagecoach Grimsby Cleethorpes depôt in June 2006. Several attempts have been made to convert the Grimsby operation to ERG in common with GCT, but the ERG is not able to store all the additional data required to accommodate the former Road Car operation. Elsewhere, the A90 continues unchallenged. Corporate titled Stagecoach rolls appeared in 2006, the only Stagecoach operation now using A90s. A casualty of this is company name no longer appears on the back of advert rolls.

Moving to Cleethorpes meant my "local" operator was **The Grimsby Cleethorpes Joint Transport Committee**. Acceptable as they wore a blue livery, my favourite bus colour, but not alas ticket wise as TIM machines were in use. Whilst having their own charm, a vast difference from the scene in Hull. This was pre Travelcards and Multiriders days. A little flutter of excitement when decimalisation came and a new batch of machines were purchased for the occasion. Subsequent replacements showed minor changes in the presentation of the title.

An Autoslot was tried issuing stock 6d "Solomatic" tickets, but when the replacement for TIMs came about in 1982, Almex E coupled to fare boxes was chosen. Like Hull earlier, the Fareboxes were deeply unpopular with passengers. Shortly before the Almex Es, in 1981, Setright Speeds were introduced on the Immingham joint service, as some return fares had risen above £1. To meet these fares with TIM meant

marriage, so twelve machines were obtained from Lincolnshire Road Car. Titled rolls were produced for these machines. Setright Speeds continued after the introduction of Almex Es. By nature of the Almex E, a crude fare structure was introduced for Grimsby local fares. Independently of this, a new image was being promoted and the new logo appeared on the tickets. But again, as with TIM, one ticket and you have got them all! Almex Es and Setright Speeds did not last long being replaced by Wayfarer 2 from 1985, following bench trails with Wayfarer 1 in 1984. Although I obtained a specimen of a Mark 1 ticket, like many other members at the time, I did not fully appreciate the storage problems of thermal tickets and this specimen is now a piece of off cream paper. Wayfarer 2 machines initially issued plain rolls but attractive titled issues did appear before the limited company was formed. As noted earlier, some of these rolls were used in Hull.

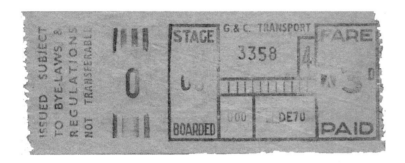

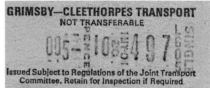

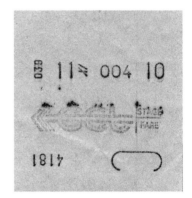

I did not see Ultimates in use, but a sympathetic inspector when I first moved to Cleethorpes took me into the loft at the depôt one evening and there were rolls of former tickets, withdrawn some eight years previously still up there. I was able to lift a roll of each value including some tailored "TRANSPORT SERVICES" issues, as well as some tokens.

In addition to conventional valued plastic tokens, specials were produced for dock workers who were required to travel from Grimsby Docks to Immingham Docks on the joint service introduced when the Grimsby & Immingham Tramway service was reduced. There were specific issues for stevedoring companies, as well as a general Grimsby Immingham Return issue. This latter token still sees limited issue, but the others fell into disuse with increasing car ownership, and an attempt to replace it with a Travelcard. Although titled GCT, tokens were valid on Road car vehicles on the joint service.

Another company to provide tokens or vouchers, this time in paper form was Laporte Industries. Until 1961 adequately served by the Grimsby & Immingham Tramway until its closure, the factory was now out on a limb regarding public transport. Some timings of the joint service were diverted to pass the works and passengers could obtain prepaid vouchers or pay normal fares. These vouchers were withdrawn in 1980 when usage fell and contract buses replaced the service. The vouchers were available for use on GCT and Road Car vehicles.

In 1981, some enlightenment occurred and a series of unlimited travel tickets burst on the scene. Multiriders allowed unlimited travel on all local GCT services but only as far as Toothill on the joint service to Immingham. Travelcards allowed unlimited travel on all services including the joint service beyond Toothill to Immingham Docks, with a cheaper version for the intermediate villages. The Travelcard was also valid on Road Car vehicles on the joint services. The

Travelcards were jointly titled BUT were not valid on any other Road Car service working into Grimsby and Cleethorpes. Initially cards were available in Adult, or Child, Weekly, Monthly or 6 monthly options. Basic principles were; background grid weekly-blue, monthly-yellow, (six monthly was met with consecutively dated monthlies), with printed text black for Adult and Red for Child. In 1984, a restricted Travelcard (if that is not a contradiction) was produced to cater for dock workers. This replaced all but one of the tokens and allowed travel between Grimsby Dock and Immingham Dock only. This version had a purple background grid.

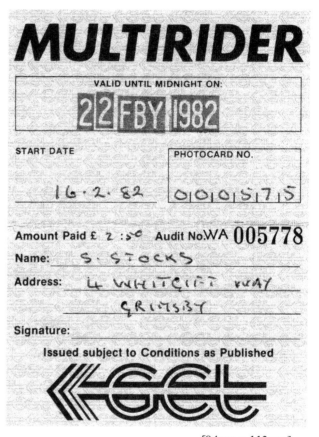

[84mm x 112mm]

The full story of the subsequent variants of these cards with deregulation, changes in local authority titles, Stagecoach and ETMs turned out to be sufficient for a talk in itself as attendees of Manchester meetings will have heard. This made up in time for the disappointment of encountering TIMs when I first came here.

In 1983, a Dayrider was offered through the summer period. Paper tickets were produced for this facility which did not prove popular, and was not repeated until ETMs arrived. These were available as Child or Family only!

1	2	3	4	5	6	7	8	9	10	11	12	13	14	15	16

DAYRIDER H & S № 00052

Family

MAY

JUNE

JULY

To date your ticket present it to the driver on
the date you wish to travel — he or she will
punch the appropriate day and month.

AUG

NOT VALID AFTER 4th SEPTEMBER, 1983

SEPT

⊠	17	18	19	20	21	22	23	24	25	26	27	28	29	30	31

[127mm x 57mm]

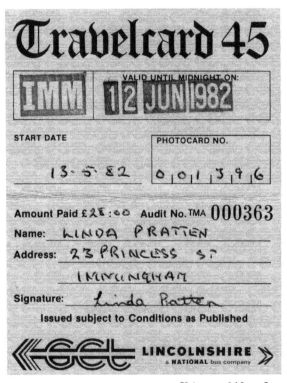

[84mm x 112mm]

Grimsby Cleethorpes Transport Co Ltd

Deregulation lead to the inevitable arms length company being established. As well as the addition of Co Ltd to the company title, some expansion took place following Road Car's abandonment of its Grimsby base. (Services still worked in from Lincoln and Louth). Travelcards were quickly reprinted. Multiriders allowed travel beyond Toothill to the actual town boundary, and to Holton le Clay on a new service to Louth in competition with Road Car. A summer service was operated to Skegness and whilst the driver was at Skegness, a service was run to the holiday camps. Allowed under deregulation, but a thorn in Road Car's side along with everybody else taking a slice of this particular cake.

Travelcards remained for the Immingham route now operated solely by GCT Co Ltd, a route that remains to this day under Stagecoach. The provision of subsidised transport by the County Councils resulted in new

cards being produced to reflect this concession. Background grid was pale blue and main text green.

Following the Stagecoach takeover of Road Car, Travelcards are now valid on the parallel service to Barton, and Road Car are able to issue Travelcards though their A90s.

Wayfarer 2 continued in use with newly titled rolls reflecting the post deregulation era. The first issue a bit insipid, but becoming orange, when that colour was adopted for the buses. A short lived facility was the Supersaver. A 12 for the price of 10 point to point ticket which generated the production of a laminated wallet. Whilst providing some interest, the limited company had nothing on what Stagecoach was going to do. In November 1993, GCT as it was still referred to locally, was acquired by Stagecoach. Legally the company is still Grimsby Cleethorpes Transport Co. Ltd.

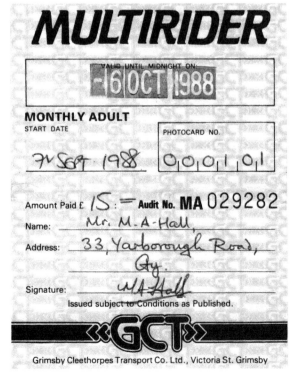

[86mm x 114mm]

48

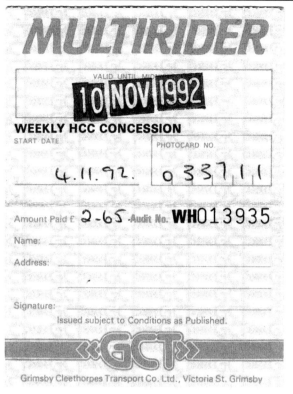

[84mm x 112mm]

things (something which Hull managed to resist for many years as we have seen). Add to this the advent of Image, Schades etc. multicoloured advertising rolls and things picked up. Advertisement rolls resulted in non standard colours, viz yellow, red.

The progression of Stagecoach branding continued with the Wayfarer's replacement, the ERG TP4000 in August 1999 and continues at the time of writing. (Some silliness when the Grimsby operation of Road Car was moved into GCT's depôt was the use of Road Car Almex A90 rolls through ERG machines. The reverse could not happen as the ERG rolls are too wide to fit the A90).

Whilst with Stagecoach, management of the company has been stand alone, then by East Midland from Chesterfield, and now Lincolnshire Road Car from Lincoln. How things come round!

Referred to as **Stagecoach in Grimsby Cleethorpes** until the end of 2007, some vehicles are now carrying the legend Stagecoach in Lincolnshire.

Wayfarers continued for normal ticket issue. However, we now get an explosion of issues as Stagecoach gradually imposed its corporate image on

[110mm x 37mm]

[110mm x 37mm]

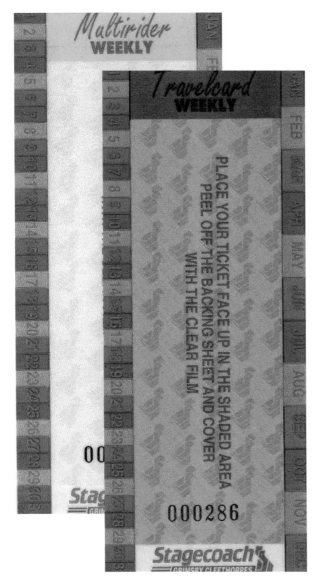

[All 140mm x 62mm]

Multiriders and Travelcards have metamorphosed through the various Stagecoach image changes. In an attempt to increase sales, the weekly versions of these cards became available as an on bus issue as well as office issues. Laminated wallets were produced from 1996 for both, being rebranded Silver or Gold Megarider respectively in 1998. Laminated wallets were withdrawn with the introduction of ERG machines, but it is still possible to purchase Silver and Gold Megariders on bus, but these are no longer encapsulated and look well worn at the end of a week. On bus issues are cheaper than office issues for the same facility, but there are some die-hards who still buy the office cards. The terms Gold and Silver have not appeared on office issue cards, but Megarider has for the former Multirider/Silver Megarider. The office issue Travelcard still uses this name. Quite apart from the antics of Stagecoach local government was re-organised yet again in 1996 and the former County of Humberside was replaced by several Unitary Authorities. Grimsby, Cleethorpes and Immingham together with a few villages became North East Lincolnshire. This change eventually manifested itself on the concessionary cards until these were withdrawn when free travel was made available to all over 60 in 2005.

The Wheatsheaf

For the 2001/2002 football season, the landlord of The Wheatsheaf public house in Grimsby came up with an idea. The Wheatsheaf is located close to Grimsby town centre and some three or so miles from Grimsby Town's football ground in Cleethorpes. He offered a Park and Ride facility, with a discount on a bar meal after the game. The vehicle used was hired from Stagecoach Peter Sheffield. Tickets were produced on a computer for each match. The scheme was not repeated in following years.

There have been other operators on the fringes of Grimsby Cleethorpes and Scunthorpe but as stated at the start, they were users of stock tickets.

RAILWAYS

Main line rail services along the South Bank were provided by the Great Central and Great Northern railways and their predecessors. New Holland, as already mentioned, became the Eastern terminus of the Great Central for a while until extended to Grimsby/Cleethorpes for passenger and Immingham for freight

The South Bank though has provided some interest in the field of small gauge and heritage rail interest. At Scunthorpe there is the **Appleby Frodingham Railway Preservation Society**. This Society has a collection of industrial locomotives and is located courtesy of Tata Steel (formerly British Steel, then Corus), within Scunthorpe Steel works. Throughout the summer, rail tours are operated around the 180 miles of internal railway including sidings at the steel works, with commentary. Pre-booking is required for security and safety reasons to control the number of visitors. A very interesting day out none the less.

[148mm x 106mm]

51

Following the closure of the former Great Northern route to London via Louth and Boston in 1970 to passenger traffic, there was talk of preserving the Grimsby to Louth section when it eventually closed to freight some ten years later. Specials were run just prior to the final closure, but funding could not be raised in time before BR started track lifting. A truncated scheme now operates, run by the Great Northern and East Lincolnshire Railway plc (t/a Lincolnshire Wolds Railway). The wish to run from Grimsby to Louth can not now be achieved as building work at Louth and a relief road at Grimsby prevent access at each end. However, the railway runs most Sundays from its base at Ludborough, about eight miles South of Grimsby. North Thoresby has not yet been reached.

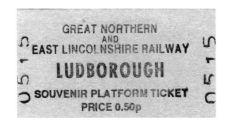

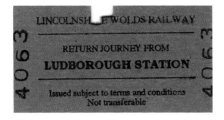

Main Line Railways

Most of my acquisitions are again from British Railways days and later so illustrations represent the less common bookings. One ticket of note is the Findus Foods Social Committee ticket to Bristol; doubly special as I was involved in arranging this day out, which included a tour of Cheddar Gorge.

Cleethorpes and Crimsby are currently very much on the Rail Tour map these days, with tours both starting and terminating at Cleethorpes.

Sun

Appleby Frodingham Railway Preservation Society

ADULT £5-00
Steam Weekend
valid on date of Issue only

Subject to the terms & conditions of AFRPS

LUDBOROUGH SAVER

LINCOLNSHIRE WOLDS RAILWAY

LUDBOROUGH TO NORTH THORESBY

This ticket is worth 50p off the price of an ordinary return to Ludborough when the line extension to North Thoresby is completed.

Date   No. 1128

We need help - track materials cost a lot of money, can you, dear customer please help us by purchasing these 25p Ludborough Savers so we can reach North Thoresby quickly.

We have the manpower and enthusiasm but lack the resources to move as quickly as we would like, but we can always do with extra help (in all departments) if you can spare a few hours.

Thank you

P.S. You can purchase as many tickets as you like!

More Ludborough Savers equals more track.
01507 363881

[115mm x 150mm]

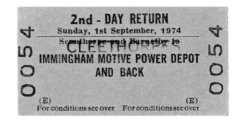

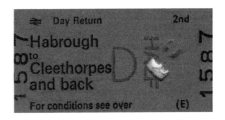

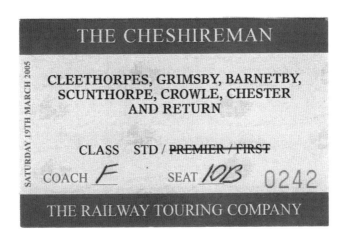

Small Gauge Railways

When I moved to Cleethorpes, I knew about the traditional miniature railway along the seafront from day trips as a youth. What I was not aware of was that there were two other miniature railways at the same time.

The traditional railway was being operated by the council, and ran for the summer season. It was started as a private venture in 1946, being taken over by the local authority in the 1950s. During its life with the Council, Edmondsons, Ultimates, Roll Tickets and self-service car park style tickets were used. Changes in title of municipal authority due to local government reorganisation are represented in the titles and the common error with regard to charging of VAT in 1974 is recorded for all to see. In 1991 this railway passed to the Cleethorpes Coast Light Railway, who operate through the summer and weekends all year round. More of them later.

The second, **The Lincolnshire Coast Light Railway** was further south than the council railway and was a commercial venture (not a preservation project) started in 1960. Rolling stock was heritage though, being industrial in origin. It provided a service from North Sea Lane to the fledgling holiday camps. Later, competition from Grimsby Cleethorpes Transport from 1967 onwards, affected traffic. During the 1970s increased car ownership further affected traffic and the fall out from the miner's strike in the early 1980s resulted in the line's closure in 1985. All is not lost though. The stock and fittings were placed into storage and are currently being re-laid at Skegness Water Park and the company had its first public open day in June 2005, but is not yet fully operational.

The three railways when my kids were young meant that at least one summer Sunday involved a ritual of walking to and travelling on all three on the same day. Not always appreciated by my offspring or long suffering, but supportive wife.

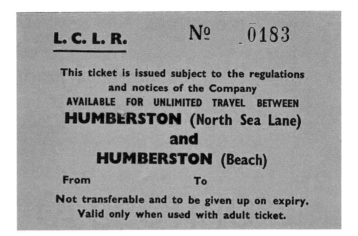

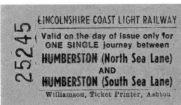

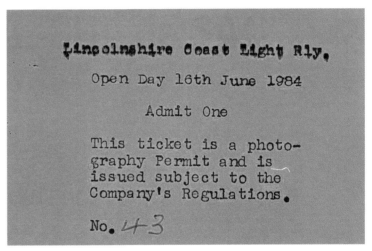

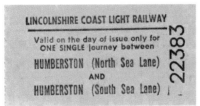

The Cleethorpes Coast Light Railway was formed in 1991 to take over the operation of the miniature railway previously operated by Cleethorpes Council. Ticket issues since then have changed and developed as the needs of the railway changed. New stations have been built although the same tickets are issued at them all. However, following the major extension in May 2007, and the introduction of "half line" fares and tickets, the tickets are now hand stamped on the reverse with the issuing station and date.

In 1992 roll tickets, printed by Thompson of Sunderland were used. The same tickets were used for Single and Return fares. A corner was cut off if issued as a Single. Adult, Child/Snr Citizen, Family, Complimentary, Dog, and Blank tickets were produced in different colours

Revised prints appeared in 1994, with separate issues for Single and Return journeys, some with text now in lower case.

1995 saw the introduction of Edmondson type cards, printed by Hacking's of Church, for all bookings with a 50p discount on the back for visits to The National Fishing Heritage Centre in Grimsby. Reprints of these tickets did not carry the Heritage Centre Promotion. By 1999, the Complimentary ticket had reverted to a roll type, by Hackings.

A change of printer to The Edmondson Ticket Printing Company produced tickets essentially the same as Hackings products, but there were differences in shade of the same colour.

In May 2007, there was a major line extension and "half line" tickets were introduced for journeys from/to either end to the middle station only. The previous tickets continued in use for the whole line journey. Tickets were now stamped with issuing

1992

1994

1995

c2000

2007

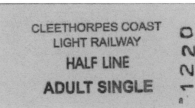

station on the reverse. Half line tickets only available for Adult or Child, Single or Return bookings. At the same time, Day Rover tickets were introduced. Whole line tickets allow a break of journey at Lakeside Station, where there is a café and tea shop.

1998 saw the introduction of a 14 journey ticket for the season. Blue and yellow are known.

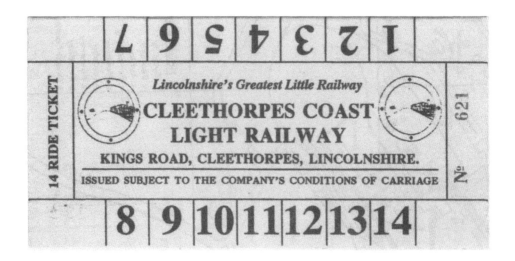

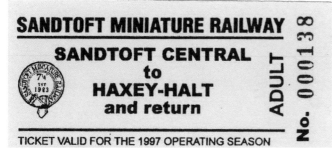

There are again three railways operating in Cleethorpes, but two are within the confines of Pleasure Island Theme Park, and can only be accessed by paying the Park entrance fee. These railways do not issue tickets in their own right.

Finally, like most areas, there is The Grimsby & Cleethorpes Model Engineering Society. This Society has been unfortunate in that until it settled on a heritage site at Waltham Windmill just outside Grimsby, it had several locations in Cleethorpes, rendering it difficult to settle and develop. Each one disappeared under building developments. The Society now operates on a substantial development at Waltham and adds to the other heritage attractions and museum being developed there. No tickets are issued for single journeys but I am ashamed that it needed Bert Ellery to dig out the fact that booklets of 10 journey tickets existed. Tickets are printed in several colours, but there is no significance in the colours used.

Away from the coast, a miniature railway operated at Sandtoft Transport Centre from 1988. Museum entrance fee had to be paid first and there was a small additional charge for the railway. The railway closed in May 2000 and has moved to Thorne.

Like Grimsby and Cleethorpes, Scunthorpe Model Engineers, who are located at Normanby Hall, have an installation, but do not issue tickets on their trains.

Confusingly tickets exist headed BOROUGH OF SCUNTHORPE/Normanby Hall/TRAIN RIDE. These are for a dotto train operating in the grounds! Cleethorpes also has a dotto train operating along the seafront. Commencing in the early 1990s titled tickets appeared by 1997. Titles have changed as the concession has changed. Tickets are roll types issued

on board with different colours from each end. The 2007 tickets are most uninspiring simply showing serial and price.

And finally, an area not touched on today is that of local authority passes and tokens for scholars, students, disabled and the elderly. During the time mainly under review this relatively small part of the country has spawned Boothferry District Council, Cleethorpes BC, Cleethorpes Town Council, East Lindsey DC, East Riding County Council, East Riding of Yorkshire Council, Glanford Brigg RDC, Great Grimsby CBC, Grimsby RDC, Haltemprice UDC, Humberside CC, Kingston-upon-Hull City Council, North East Lincolnshire Council, Scunthorpe BC, West Lindsey DC, etc, though not all at the same time.

Well gentlemen, I thank you for putting up with my ramblings, but it does show you do not need a London, Manchester, Glasgow or Greenock to dig out some desirable items for your collection.

In closing I thank the following for their assistance in preparation of this presentation.

R. Atkinson
B. G. Boddy
W. A. Brinkley
P. J. Smith

Grimsby Archive Offices
Hull Local Studies Library
K.H.C.T. 1899-1979, K.H.C.T.
Lincolnshire and East Yorkshire Transport Review (and predecessors)
PSV Circle
Transport Ticket Society (and predecessors) *Journal*

Thank you,

Ken Pudsey